Shields Up!
Complete Guide to Windows Security and Mac Privacy

LIZ CORNWELL

Table of Contents

Disclaimer

The information presented herein represents the views of the author as of the date of publication. Because of the rate with which conditions change, the author reserves the rights to alter and update their opinions accordingly.

This book is for informational purposes only and the author is not to be held responsible for any liabilities resulting from the use of this information. While every effort has been made to verify the information provided in this book, the author and her resellers and affiliates cannot assume any responsibility for errors, inaccuracies or omissions. Any slights of people or organizations are unintentional.

Foreword

Computers have changed the way we live. Everywhere you look, you will see someone using a laptop, a smartphone or a tablet PC. We use computers to communicate, to work, to study, to unleash our creativity, to get entertainment, to shop, to do banking – the list goes on and on. There are thousands of advantages to using computers. However, there is one great hazard that puts every single user at risk – security threats.

Put it simply, we all want to be confident that we are safe when we use our computers and when we connect to the Internet. Unfortunately, the convenience of using computers and the Web comes at a cost, as there are hundreds of infections, scams and other threats.

Viruses, malware, online fraud, identity theft, hacker attacks and more – all these things can happen to you when you are using the Internet. That's because the Internet is still uncensored and thus is pretty much unregulated. To me, this is one of the wonderful things about the Internet that I love. But, if I'm honest, the Internet can become your worst enemy if your computer gets infected and your privacy gets compromised. What you need to understand is that it's your responsibility to keep your computer protected. No one but you can watch out for suspicious stuff on the Web, protect your files and avoid online fraud. Remember that there are no policemen to keep you safe.

The first thing you need to understand is that keeping your computer and your online accounts safe is more than installing an anti-virus program and forgetting all about it. Computer security is a process, not a piece of software that can do everything for you in the background.

Keeping your data safe is a constant battle that we all have to fight on a daily basis. I'm not saying this to scare you - I simply want you to understand that you have to stay alert and remember a basic set of rules that you must follow at all times.

If you like, you can compare computer security with driving. Driving seems awfully hard when you are just starting and there seem to be way too many rules to remember. However, once you get some experience, it becomes almost as natural as walking. But one thing never changes: you always need to remember the rules and you need to keep your eyes open for anything unusual and potentially dangerous. Same with computer security. Once you know what to watch out for, staying safe becomes a lot easier than you may first think.

In this book, I'm going to explain how different computer infections and online threats work and what you can do to protect yourself. I will show you how to avoid computer infections, stay away from online fraud and identity theft, secure your home network and protect yourself from hacker attacks. I will also teach you how to protect your online privacy and make sure that no one but you can access your personal information. Plus I'm going to recommend some handy software you can use to improve the security of your PC or Mac.

"Shields Up! Complete Guide to Windows Security and Mac Privacy" will arm you with fundamental knowledge that will help you and your data stay safe both online and offline.

The Basics of Computer Security

System Protection and the Latest Threats

Computer security has been an issue ever since computers became a part of our lives. Viruses and malware are here to stay. When the first viruses emerged, they weren't a major concern, but these days security threats are developing at an alarming rate. New infections are created daily, which means that anti-virus software manufacturers struggle to keep up with them. In addition to new infections, there are threats that have the potential to do a lot more harm than any virus. I mean threats like identity theft, online fraud, and countless scams. Even governments realize the dangers of malware and online threats, hence all the different regulations designed to protect both consumers and businesses.

Unfortunately, regulations don't really work when it comes to online threats because the Web lives according to its own laws. But there are many things you can do to protect your computer, your bank account and your identity.

The key to protecting yourself from viruses, malware, identity theft, scams and other dangers of the Web is understanding how they work. You need to know your enemy to be able to defend yourself. In this chapter I'm going to explain the basics of computer security and tell you about the latest and the most dangerous threats.

Key points of system security

So, what is a secure system and what makes a system secure? This question sounds difficult to computer novices, but in reality it's pretty easy to answer. To cut a long story short, a secure system is a system that has:

• Secure and controlled user access
• Personal information protection
• Real-time protection
• Secure backups

This list doesn't include every possible security measure, but it covers the minimum needed to protect a home computer. Let's have a closer look at these points.

Secure and controlled user access

When you switch your computer on, one of the first things you see is a user log on screen where you enter your username and password. Unless you have password protection disabled, you would not be able to go any further without logging in. While a lot of people find this procedure unnecessary and time-consuming, your user account password is your first shield. Your password is the first barrier an intruder has to pass when trying to hack into your system. That's why it's so important to have a strong system login password that no one but you can easily figure out.

Personal information protection

Protecting your personal information is essential to having a secure system and avoiding disasters like identity theft. Data is protected by everyone – governments issue data protection acts, financial institutions are required by law to protect their clients' information and their own financial data, even schools protect the personal information of their pupils.

Despite all these protection measures, identity theft is becoming a huge problem. Every year more and more ordinary people have their identity stolen mostly by people who get loans and credit cards in other people's names. That's why it's essential to protect your personal information as best you can. A good start is getting an anti-virus, installing a reliable firewall and using encryption software to protect important files like bank statements, tax returns, and other files that contain your confidential information and can attract hackers.

We will talk more about secure system access in the next chapter where I'll tell you how to make sure only you can access your system and your data. And now let's move on to real-time protection and see what it is, how it works, and how it can help you.

Real-time protection

Protecting your files and folders with anti-virus and encryption programs is good, but it's not enough. That's because a lot of security software can only recognize malicious code by its signature.

Ever noticed your anti-virus updating daily? When the software is doing that, it's not updating itself, but rather downloading new virus definitions that are issued every day, sometimes several times a day. Sounds good, doesn't it? Well, there is one problem. Literally hundreds of viruses, Trojans and other malicious programs are developed every day. And anti-virus programs cannot possibly keep track of them all. This means that you always risk getting infected by something that is called a "zero-day threat" – a malicious program that has just been released. Malware like that can't be detected by its signature simply because there are no signatures for it yet. That's where real-time protection comes to rescue.

Real-time protection is a security software feature that can detect even the most recent viruses and malware. Malicious programs are identified based on their behavior rather than their signature. Basically, the anti-virus program monitors everything that happens on your computer and checks all running processes to see if anything weird is going on. For example, if a suspicious process tries to edit the registry or connect to the Internet, the user gets notified by the security software. Monitoring your PC activity for zero-day threats is essential if you want to have a secure system. This is especially relevant if you use your computer for work and need to pay extra attention to security. Zero-day threats often try to get access to your data and not having a behavioral scanner to stop it can result in all your client data getting compromised.

Real-time protection feature is present in most modern anti-virus packages, but you can always install a separate behavioral scanner for an extra layer of security.

Secure backups

Most people don't typically associate system backups with computer security. In a way they are right - backups have very little to do with viruses and malware. And yet having a recent backup can one day become your lifesaver.

Imagine this: your computer gets infected with a nasty virus. A virus so nasty that and the only way to remove the infection is to reformat the hard drive. Reformatting means that all your files, folders, programs, and your operating system will be gone. Unless you have everything backed up. If you have a backup, you will be able to restore all your stuff in no time.

But there is one problem with some types of backups. If you back up your files to a thumb drive or an external hard drive, all your data can be stolen or lost if you lost the drive. That's why the most secure way to create a complete system backup is disk imagining (taking a snapshot of your system) and secure encrypted online backup of your files.

Disk imaging is only good if your system was virus-free when the backup was created. Otherwise the virus will be restored along with everything else and you'll end up having to reformat again. That's why I store my backups in the cloud. There are plenty of cloud backup providers. I've used Backblaze and Carbonite, but you are welcome to do your own research and find the provider you like best. The important thing is that you find a backup solution that is easy to use, works well on all your devices, and uses encryption to keep your data safe.

These are the basics of computer security. But you might be asking why you need to pay so much attention to PC security and backups. The answer is simple - because there are hundreds of threats out there and your system may be vulnerable to attacks. So, let's have a look at system vulnerabilities and discuss the most common threats.

Vulnerabilities

When you think of computer security, three key points come to mind: vulnerabilities, threats and protective measures. I'm sure you know at least something about threats and protective measures. But what are vulnerabilities? Time for some theory.

A vulnerability is a point in your system that is most exposed to attacks. Potentially, every single computer or network is vulnerable to attacks. No matter which security products you have installed, there is always a chance to get infected one way or another. The goal of computer security products is to find vulnerabilities and protect your system from possible attacks.

There are different types of system vulnerabilities because a vulnerability can occur anywhere in the system. Here are the most common ones that you need to watch out for:

• **Hardware vulnerabilities** – it's not a secret that hardware, especially hard drives, can fail. That's pretty nasty, but thankfully hard drive failures don't compromise computer security. Don't get me wrong, losing your data because of a hard disk failure is bad, but at least it's not as bad as getting your data stolen by hackers. Unfortunately, there are other types of hardware failures that can open security holes and make it really easy for hackers to lay their hands on your data and use external devices to copy your private information. To protect yourself from hardware faults, keep your drivers and firmware updated and remember to upgrade your hardware every once in a while.

• **Operating system and software vulnerabilities** – these vulnerabilities are the most common and the most dangerous ones. Malware developers constantly test operating systems and other software for weak spots. When they find one, they take advantage of it and develop malware that can infect the system using that particular vulnerability. Luckily, keeping your operating system and software fully patched usually helps to avoid getting infected because Microsoft and other software manufacturers release security patches and hotfixes as quickly as they can.

An overview of security threats

Now you know what vulnerabilities are, it's time to get some insight into security threats. The Web is full of them. Some of them are unintentional, but most are created with the purpose of jeopardizing your computer security either for fun or in an attempt to access your bank details and steal your money.

All infections and hacking attempts are different and they often need to be dealt with in different ways. To fight various security threats, you need to know what they are and how they affect your computer. Here is an overview of the most common security and privacy threats:

• **Malware** – short for malicious software, malware is software designed to compromise computers. For example, malware can disrupt or deny operations, collect the user's private information for identity theft purposes, gain unauthorized access to various system components, and behave in an abusive manner. Basically, malware is a general term used by professionals to describe malicious, intrusive and hostile software or code.

• **Computer virus** – this is the best-known security threat. A virus is a small piece of software that is written with the purpose to alter your computer settings and change the way your computer operates. It's called a virus because it can reproduce itself and infect other PCs. Funnily enough, the first viruses were harmless and all they did was reproduce.

• **Trojan horse** – just like the Trojan horse in Greek mythology, computer Trojan horses pretend to be harmless. But in reality they get inside your system and perform destructive actions.

- **Computer worm** – worms are one of the most dangerous pieces of malware. They use the network to copy themselves to other computers and they do so without the user's knowledge.

- **Rootkit** – the most dangerous and hard to remove piece of malware. Rootkits infect various system components, but most of the time they target the kernel, firmware and user applications.

- **Spyware** – basically, spyware are programs that spy on the user and collect small pieces of information.

- **Adware** – this is perhaps the most annoying malicious software. If you've ever had annoying pop-ups appear out of nowhere even when you are not connected to the Internet, you know what I mean. Adware is any software that automatically displays or downloads advertisements. Adware alone is usually harmless, however it's often integrated with spyware, keyloggers and malware. That's why most anti-malware and anti-spyware programs are designed to protect you from adware as well.

- **Ransomware** – this type of malicious software has become very popular in recent years. Ransomware acts like human blackmail because it either locks you out of your computer (or accounts) or threatens to publish your private data unless you pay the ransom. Usually, cybercriminals who use ransomware ask for a lot of money, especially if the victim of their attack is a large organization. Most of the time, the blackmailers ask for payments in cryptocurrencies because such transactions are difficult to trace. Unfortunately, paying up doesn't guarantee that the criminals will keep their promise. CryptoWall, WannaCry, Petya and Bad Rabbit are some of the most recent examples of ransomware attacks.

The latest security threats

For the last couple of years online malicious activity has been the major security threat. Various scams have been appearing on Facebook and Twitter, and even Google Play gets infected every now and again. In addition to that, the world saw a number of politically motivated hacker attacks. But these are not a threat to the average home computer user, so we won't concentrate on them. It's the other online security threats you need to know about, so that you can stay away from them.

Because most of these threats are new and don't use traditional methods, security software can't really help you fight them. Besides, no security software can protect you from elaborate scams. Your common sense is usually the best weapon against scams and even against infections.

So, keep your eyes open and don't let fake anti-viruses, social network scams, infected email attachments or fake emails from your bank fool you and result in things like identity theft, stolen bank details or even plain old burglars breaking into your house.

Let's have a look at the latest security threats and see how you can avoid them.

Social network scams

Social networks, like Facebook, Google+ and Twitter, are becoming more and more popular. They are great for connecting with friends, getting the most recent news and even finding a job. Unfortunately, not everybody uses social networks for legitimate purposes – various scams and other social network threats breed like mice.

Facebook is a lot more dangerous than Twitter because of various apps and games. Believe it or not, but studies by BitDefender show that as much as 20% of Facebook users are active targets of malware. And this number is growing.

Most social network scams are phishing attacks where you are invited to check out a link that supposedly comes from a friend. The scammers try to lure you with cool photos or videos that you "absolutely have to check out". When you click on the link, your personal information is collected and sent to the hacker. Some links install malware on your PC in the process.

You might think that it's no big deal if some of your Facebook information gets stolen. But if your Facebook profile has information like your date of birth, location, cell phone number and email address, hackers can create fake profiles using that information and even steal your identity. On top of that, your profile can get infected and you will become a zombie who actually spreads the scam. Not a good scenario. And, of course, there are Facebook apps that install malicious software on your computer.

The best way to protect yourself from such scams is to think twice before clicking on a link, even if it comes from a friend. If someone is telling you to check out a cool photo or video in a suspicious manner and the link appears shortened (like bit.ly), don't click on it immediately, but ask your friend if they sent you the link or not.

Also never install unknown apps, as they may be infected. If you think that your profile might already be infected, the first thing to do is change your password and revoke the access for any suspicious apps.

Another threat is plain and simple burglary that gets committed based on what you say on Facebook and Twitter. You see, criminals browse social networks for posts about people going on holiday. When burglars find profiles that have a status message like "Going to New York for the weekend!" and personal details like home address or phone number, they know exactly when it's safe to break into your house. And it will be entirely your fault because you practically invited them in.

Countering burglary and identity theft on Facebook is pretty easy – don't post your personal information. Your friends know how old you are and they know where you live. They also know your cell phone number.

So really, there is no need to post all this information on Facebook. Just like you won't be writing your details on walls and printing them on your T-shirt for the world to see, you shouldn't post them all over the Internet. And never broadcast information about when you are planning to go on holidays or trips – there are plenty of other ways to let your friends and family know.

Mobile apps

Mobile apps are another big thing – everybody has smartphones and everybody likes downloading and trying out different apps. After all, there are hundreds of really useful or fun apps for both iOS and Android devices. Unfortunately, quite a few mobile apps are malicious. This is especially true for Android apps.

These apps can be pretty nasty, like DroidDream. Luckily, Google was able to stop it, but it caused a lot of harm. The DroidDream app allowed malware to get administrative access to people's phones, so that it could install more malware and steal their personal data. Since most people store a lot of important and confidential information on their phones, DroidDream caused quite a bit of trouble.

Even though Google Play now uses a service called Bouncer to automatically scan all apps for malware, it can't fully guarantee that all apps are malware-free. So, just like with social media scams, the best way to protect yourself is to use your common sense.

Never download unknown applications, no matter how attractive they sound. Always check user reviews before you download anything and check permissions the app requires before you agree to install it. If you are on a corporate phone, you should also consider installing an anti-virus for your Android. There many options available for download on Google Play, including Android security solutions from well-known software developers like BitDefender, Avast, AVG and so on.

If you are an iOS user, you are safer because Apple's App Store does a better job at detecting and banning malicious apps. However, some infections slipped through in the past, so it's always good to check and double-check an app before installing it.

Fake anti-virus programs

Fake anti-viruses are not a novelty anymore, yet thousands of people still become victims. In fact, fake anti-virus scams are on the rise and become more and more elaborate.

Basically, people are fooled by bogus alerts that their computer is infected and they need to purchase the anti-virus to delete the infection. Unsuspecting users get scared (hence these bogus programs are also called "scareware") and immediately grab their credit card to pay for the bogus software. But paying doesn't stop the problem – on the contrary, the money gets stolen, more malware is installed on the computer, and the culprits have your bank card details so that they can potentially drain your account. Keep in mind that fake registry cleaner alerts work in a similar way, so watch out for them too.

Protecting yourself from fake anti-virus programs is not easy because getting the pop-up usually means that you are already infected. So the best thing is to have an anti-virus with good real-time protection. Keep your security software up-to-date and give your computer regular scans. Also never enter your financial details into pop-up windows that appear out of nowhere. If a suspicious pop-up appears, don't click on it and run an anti-virus scan immediately.

PDF attachments

Sending malware in email attachment has always been a popular distribution method. Even though Web email providers like Gmail, Yahoo and Hotmail scan all attachments for viruses, some infections get missed.

PDF has proven to be the most dangerous file format because PDF infections are easy to generate and are even easier to mask as legitimate documents. To avoid getting infected through PDF files, never open any attachments from unknown senders. Even if the PDF comes from a friend, it's good to download it and scan it with your anti-virus software before opening.

Also don't forget to keep Adobe Reader fully patched – Adobe keeps track of vulnerabilities and attempts to release timely hotfixes.

But in fact, it's a good idea to ditch Adobe Reader altogether and replace it with Foxit Reader, a free PDF viewing and form filling tool that's a lot more secure than Adobe Reader and has a lot of cool and useful features.

Now you have some idea about the threats that lurk around. So, let's make sure that your computer stays safe and secure. And the first thing to do is ensure secure system access.

Friend or Foe?

How to Ensure Secure System Access

When we think of computer security, most of us start thinking of various anti-virus programs and complicated Facebook passwords. We almost never think of secure and controlled system access. And that's a big mistake because neglecting setting up secure system access can lead to a disaster.

The first question I'm going to ask you is who can log into your system? Most likely, the answer is anyone because too many home PCs and laptops are not protected in any way. Do you get your desktop screen a few seconds after pressing the power button? If yes, then you don't even have a password that makes access to your computer more or less secure.

If your computer doesn't ask you for a password when you turn it on, then a feature called automatic login is enabled. This speeds up computer boot, but jeopardizes security, as it removes an important security barrier that is there to protect your computer from physical unauthorized access. Basically, auto login lets anyone log into your computer.

Are you prepared to put your privacy and security at risk simply because you don't feel like waiting for a couple of seconds? If the answer is "No", let's change some Windows settings and disable automatic login.

Windows 7, 8 and 10 have automatic login disabled by default, which means that you'll have to enter a password every time you want to use your computer unless you change the settings yourself.

But if you are still using XP, you'll need to do it manually.

Here is how:

1.   Click on **Start**, click on **Run**, type **control userpasswords2** in the **Run** box and press **Enter**

2.　　In the **User Accounts** window, select the **Users must enter a user name and password to use this computer** checkbox to disable automatic login

3.　　Click **Apply**, then click **OK** and you are done

Now an unauthorized user will face the challenge of figuring out or obtaining your password to access your computer. But there's a lot more you can do to ensure that no hacker can log on to your computer even if it gets lost or stolen.

Use a restricted user account

By default, your home computer logs you on as Administrator. That's great for when you need to change various system settings and perform some system maintenance, but it's not all that great from the security point of view. You see, accessing your system using the admin account all the time means that if your computer gets infected by a Trojan, a keylogger or a rootkit, their master (the hacker) will gain full access to your computer. Definitely something you don't want to happen. That's why it's recommended that you keep your administrator account safe and use a restricted user account or even a guest account for day-to-day computer use.

A restricted user account will allow you to use your computer pretty much in the same way you've been using it. However, there will be restrictions on changing system settings, installing and uninstalling software, editing the Windows registry and accessing restricted files. All right, so you'll need to log off and log in as administrator to perform some tasks and install/uninstall some software, but your system will be a lot more secure.

Here is how you can create a restricted user account:

Windows XP:

1.   Make sure that you are logged in as administrator
2.   Click on the **Start** button and go to **Control Panel**

3.　　　Double-click on **User Accounts**

4.　　　Click on **Create a user account**
5.　　　Enter the name for the account and click **Next**

6.   Now select the **Restricted account** radio button and click on **Create user account**

Windows 7:

If you are using Windows 7, then you can configure a limited user account. Together with UAC, this will help you protect your system from any unauthorized changes to the settings. When configuring a limited user account in Windows 7, it's important to create a new account for day-to-day work and not modify your admin rights account. Otherwise you are running the risk of locking yourself out of your computer.

To create a limited user account, do the following:

1.   Log in using your administrative account
2.   Click on **Start** and go to the **Control Panel**

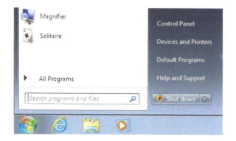

3.   Under **User Accounts and Family Safety** click on **Add or remove user accounts**

4.   Under the list of current accounts, click on **Create a new account**

5.   Type in a user name and select the **Standard user** radio button

Name the account and choose an account type

This name will appear on the Welcome screen and on the Start menu.

| User |

◉ Standard user
Standard account users can use most software and change system settings that do not affect other users or the security of the computer.

6.   Click on the **Create Account** button and you are done

Windows 8:

1.   Press **Windows + W** to open **Settings**

2.   On the **Settings** screen, click on **Users** and then select the **Add a user** option

3. A new screen will appear where you will be asked to enter the new user's email address.

4.   If you don't want to enter the email, you can click on **Sign in without a Microsoft account**

5. Click on **Local account** and then on **Next**. Confirm that you want to create a **Local account**

6.   Enter the new user's username and password

7.   Use the **Password hint** box to set up a password reminder

8. Click **Next** and Windows will create a new account. Windows 8 allows you to have only one administrator account so all other accounts are restricted.

9.   If you are creating a new account for a child, check the **Is this a child's account?** checkbox

10.   Click **Finish** and you are done

Windows 10:

1.   Press the Windows icon (the Start button) and go to **Settings**

2.   Go to **Accounts** and select **Family & other users**

3.　　Under **Other users**, click on **Add someone else to this PC**

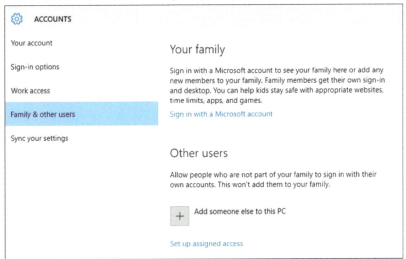

4.　　Select **I don't have this person's sign-in information** and then **Add a user without a Microsoft account**

5.　　Enter a user name, a password and a password hint to help you remember it in case you forget it, and click **Next**

Now you can use this account for day-to-day tasks, which will help you protect your system from any unauthorized changes.

Creating strong passwords

This may seem funny, but thousands of people still use "123456" as their password. However, this is no laughing matter because using weak passwords means that you are pretty much not using a password at all.

A weak obvious password doesn't take long to figure out even by amateurs and teenagers, not to mention more or less professional hackers. That's why it's essential to create strong passwords and keep changing them every now and again, for example once a month.

When creating a strong password, you need to remember two golden rules:

1. Combine letters, numbers and symbols
2. Use lowercase and uppercase

You might think that these passwords will be impossible to remember, especially when you use symbols, but that's not so. Let me give you an example how you can create a strong password that is easy to remember.

A method I quite like is using first letters of a sentence that means something to you but doesn't mean anything to anyone else as your password. For example, let's create a password using this sentence:

"When I was 14, I lived in San Diego, CA."

The password will look like this:

W!w14!liSDCA

What I did was use the first letter of each word, but I've substituted "I" with "!" – a similar enough symbol for you to remember. And since that sentence means something to you, you are not likely to forget it. Besides, there will be no harm writing the sentence down, as nobody will know that you use it as your password. Which brings us to the next topic – how to protect your passwords.

Protecting your password

Even though passwords are designed to protect you, they can get stolen. This means you need to protect your passwords. Otherwise they can be used by anyone and the consequences can be extremely damaging. So, here are some tips that will help you protect your passwords:

• Never share your passwords with anyone and never send them via email, IM, SMS, or social network email systems. Emailed and sent passwords can be easily intercepted by hackers.
• Never-ever write down your passwords, credit card PIN codes and other information that can be used against you. If you feel that you need to write that information down, use encryption software like

SensiGuard to encrypt the document where you store your passwords. Or use password management software like **LastPass** or **RoboForm**. These programs will remember your passwords and let you enter them without having to type them. This will secure your information even if your computer is infected with a keylogger - a piece of malware that records your keystrokes. RoboForm and LastPass work on Windows, Mac and support mobile operating systems.

• If there are any test passwords or passwords issued by manufacturers, change them immediately. Passwords like "test" are ridiculously easy to figure out.

• Don't type your password while someone is watching, especially if you are using a public or an office computer.

• Don't use the same password for different accounts.

• Keep changing your passwords every once in a while. Once a month is usually enough.

Remember that your password is the first barrier that protects you from intruders. Don't neglect using passwords, remember to change them regularly and don't share them with anyone, even with your friends.

Using authentication devices

One of the easiest ways to make your system access more secure is to use authentication devices.

Basically, an authentication device is a key you use to access your computer, just like you use keys to open your house or start your car. The key creates an extra security barrier and prevents unauthorized access. Yes, keys can get stolen and professional hackers can still break into your PC without the key, but it's still good to have one. It's like burglars can break into your house even if they don't have the keys, but it takes time, effort and extra skill.

So, let's have a look at your authentication devices options. There are a lot of devices that can be used for authentication purposes, but the most popular ones are smart cards (not to be confused with SD memory cards) and specially configure USB thumb drives.

Smart cards

Smart cards are any pocket-sized cards with built-in chips. Remember the chip in your bank card? Well, that's a smart card. But in this book we'll only talk about smart cards that are used for computer security purposes.

In computer security smart cards can be used for a variety of purposes, but mainly to either ensure secure system access or store protected data. For example, Mozilla Firefox can use smart cards to store certificates that are used in secure Web browsing.

Encryption software is also compatible with smart cards and uses them to securely store encryption keys and provide an extra security layer to critical parts of the encrypted disk. But most of the time smart cards are used for secure user authentication and login.

Most smart cards that are used for secure system log in are cryptographic smart cards. They use special cryptographic hardware and advanced encryption algorithms, such as RSA and DSA. Smart cards are used by a lot of businesses because they ensure secure system access, provide easy ATM-like experience for the end users, and can provide passwords for general system and software access as well as one-time password tokens for remote access.

Modern operating systems have the necessary services to support smart cards, which means that you can use them on your home or office computer provided you get a smart card reader.

USB thumb drives

Another way to ensure secure system access is to use a USB thumb drive as an authentication token. USB tokens are specially programmed USB thumb drives that have the same functionality as smart cards, but combine it with ease of use and look less obvious. Using a USB thumb drive as a login key is a secure yet cost-effective way of boosting system access security.

Another way to use a USB thumb drive for secure system access is to encrypt and store your login password on a USB drive. To do that, you'll need to use encryption software like SensiGuard or Encrypto. Encryption software protects your password by scrambling it so that it can't be read unless it's decrypted. And since 256-AES encryption is very difficult to crack, your password and other encrypted data stay safe.

These devices boost system access control a great deal. The only problem is that they can be stolen along with your computer, which will render them useless and provide the intruder with a tool for easy access to your system. That's why computer manufacturers came up with a more complicated way for users to access their computers. I'm talking about fingerprint authentication and face verification features, i.e. biometric authentication.

Biometric authentication

Biometric authentication is one of the most secure system access methods. That's because no one but you can have your fingerprints, pass a retina and iris scan for you, or match your facial features. Well, OK – your identical twin can pass the facial features test, but no one else can.

Biometric system authentication devices compare your particular traits with the data stored for you and determine your identity. This makes biometric authentication very secure and reliable. And it's not too expensive either – a lot of laptop manufacturers make laptops with fingerprint scanners and face recognition utilities.

The only flaw of biometric authentication is that if something goes wrong with the device or face verification software, you might never be able to access your computer again.

Multifactor authentication

Now you know that biometric authentication is one of the most secure system access methods. But do you know which login method will give you the ultimate system access security? Well, the answer is pretty simple and logical – it's multifactor authentication.

Multifactor authentication is an authentication method that combines two of the methods mentioned above – an authentication device and biometric authentication. This login method creates a double barrier that a user needs to pass before system access is granted. This way even if the hacker manages to get past one barrier, there is still one more and passing it is really difficult.

Conventional passwords are not really needed when the system requires multifactor authentication because a password is the weakest security measure and can be easily cracked.

Of course, multifactor authentication is a bit too extreme for a home system, but businesses that deal with confidential information usually implement multifactor system authentication.

Now you know how to create strong passwords, how to keep them safe and how to ensure secure access to your system. Let's move on and see what you can do to protect your home network.

Protect Your Environment

Home Network and Wireless Security

These days most people use Wi-Fi in their homes. Having a home network has a lot of advantages – if you have a laptop, you can use it from anywhere in your house, you are not restricted by any cables, and you can have several devices (computers, media players, mobile phones, game consoles, TV boxes etc.) connected to the Internet at once. Not to mention that having Wi-Fi installed in your house doesn't cost anything as most ISPs (Internet service providers) give you a router for free when you subscribe to a plan.

However, a Wi-Fi home network has a significant disadvantage - it's not as secure as a traditional wired connection. If you plug a cable into your computer, it's next to impossible for someone to hook to your network and steal your bandwidth. But a Wi-Fi signal can easily be used by someone within its range.

Just think of it – your neighbor could be using your connection for free while you are paying for it and so can a person in a parked car just outside your door. Not good, eh? And believe me, this is not the worst bit. After all, if you are on an unlimited plan, it doesn't matter all that much if someone else is using your connection. Of course, it's different if you don't have an unlimited plan. And in any case, having your bandwidth stolen usually means lower browsing speed for yourself.

But the worst bit is that someone can steal more than your bandwidth if they manage to connect to your network. A skilled individual will manage to access files on your computer through your own insecure network – all they need is a bit of know-how and special software. Starts sounding like someone almost breaking into your house, doesn't it?

Worse still, a hacked Wi-Fi network can even get you arrested. How? Simple. A lot of people had problems with the law for sending hate emails, spam and taking parts in scams. In reality, they did no such thing – their email accounts got hacked via an insecure home network. Definitely something you wouldn't want happening to you.

Luckily, there are ways to protect your home network from intruders and keep your private data safe without going through too much trouble. Here is how.

Don't keep your router always on

In the days of wired Internet connections, switching off your computer meant that Internet got switched off too. But using routers changed that and now most people leave their routers on even if they are not using the Internet. While it is convenient to have an always-on Internet connection, it's also pretty dangerous because hackers target such connections more often. If your connection is not on all the time, it's more difficult for hackers to hook up to it. So, if you can, switch your router off if you are not using it and if your system doesn't demand an always-on Internet connection. Doing this will make you less attractive to hackers.

Make sure your router has a good firewall

The next step is to check whether your router has a good firewall or not. A firewall is something that lets the good stuff in and keeps the nasty stuff out. There are software and hardware firewalls, the hardware ones being a lot harder to penetrate. Ideally, you should have both.

When your ISP provides you with a router, check whether it has a hardware firewall. If not, it makes sense to purchase a more expensive Cisco or Netgear router that has built-in hardware firewall functionality.

Create a unique password for your router

The first thing you need to do is make sure your router uses a secure password. Most routers come with default usernames and passwords that can be easily looked up on the Internet. So, even if there is a password that you need to enter to access the Internet, it doesn't mean you are protected.

To change your router's password and other settings, you need to access the Settings page for your router. For most brands, you can do this by typing **192.168.1.1** in your browser's address bar and entering your current username and password. Different routers have different Settings page addresses, so check your router's user manual for the correct address. Alternatively, simply go to your router's manufacturer website.

Once you are logged in on the Settings page, you can change the settings for your router. The first thing you should change is your username and password. This is usually done from the **Administration** page. Make sure you pick a unique username and create a strong password, as it will prevent intruders from breaking in.

Do not use any of your other usernames or passwords because doing so will compromise the security of more than your router configuration page.

Change the SSID name for your network

When Wi-Fi is installed in your house, the newly created network gets a default name (SSID). This name depends on your router's manufacturer and sometimes on the ISP you use. For example, it can say Verizon or Linksys.

Changing the network's SSID is a good idea because it will make it obvious for your neighbors that it's not theirs (some people use other people's Wi-Fi by accident. Not everybody is a hacker, you know). You can also change your network's name in such a way that your neighbors will be scared to touch it.

Here is how you can change your network's SSID:

1.   Log into your router's settings and find where you can change the SSID. This depends on the router brand you are using, but usually you can change the SSID under **Basic Settings**

2.   Follow the instructions to change the network's name. **DO NOT** use your name, address or anything that allows others to identify you

3.   And now the fun part. Change your network's name to something like **virus.exe** or **c:\trojan.exe**. Your neighbors or anyone who is not a techie will never touch a network called a virus!

Filter MAC addresses

No matter which device you are using to access the Internet through a home Wi-Fi network, it has a MAC (Media Access Control) address.

MAC address has nothing to do with Apple Mac – it's something similar to an IP address, which is used by every computer connected to the Internet. A MAC address is unique to each device.

Your router allows you to see the MAC addresses of all connected devices, so that you can see if an intruder is using your connection. But it gets better and better – you can add the MAC addresses for all your devices to your router's settings, so that no other devices will be able to connect to the Internet via your network. This is called MAC address filtering.

To switch on MAC address filtering, you need to decide which devices you want to connect to your network. I recommend making a list. When that's done, you'll need to find the MAC addresses of your devices. Let me show you how.

For PCs:

1.   Click on the **Start** button, then type **cmd** in the **Search bar** and press **Enter** (XP users will need to type **cmd** in the **Run...** box and hit **Enter**)

2.   The Command Prompt will open. Type **ipconfig /all** and hit **Enter**. You will get a bunch of information about your Internet connection. The **MAC address** should be under **Physical Address**

3.   Make a note of your MAC address and close the Command Prompt

For mobile devices:

1.   Go to **Settings** and then open **Network Settings** under **Wireless Networks**

2.   The MAC address should be listed there.

Now go to your router's settings and find the item that refers to MAC filtering. Sometimes it's called **Connection Control** or **MAC Address Filtering**. Then enter the MAC addresses for your devices in the fields on the page and save your settings. Reboot your router and your devices for the changes to take effect.

This will prevent any other devices from connecting to your Wi-Fi network.

If you're using your mobile phone or tablet as a Wi-Fi hotspot, then blocking other devices is really easy because you usually get a "Block" button next to each MAC address.

Enable network encryption

The best way to protect your wireless network and prevent other people from using your signal is to encrypt it. There are quite a few wireless encryption methods – WEP (Wired Equivalent Privacy), WPA (Wi-Fi Protected Access) and WPA2 (Wi-Fi Protected Access version 2).

WEP is the most basic and the least secure encryption method of them all. Hackers can easily crack it using free software like AirCrack (anyone can download it). If you are confident that your neighbors won't try to hack your connection using any advanced methods, then WEP should be enough to protect your home network. However, it's not really enough to offer strong security. The advantage of WEP is that it has been around for a long while and is compatible with all sorts of hardware.

WPA2 is the latest and the most secure signal encryption method. I strongly recommend using WPA2 if your hardware is compatible. If not, go for WEP and create a really strong password.

You can enable encryption for your home network by going to your router's configuration page and editing the settings. Different routers have different configuration pages, but it's really easy to enable either WPA2 or WEP.

Just a note. When you are done configuring your router's settings, you will need to add the new settings to all devices that connect to the Internet via your Wi-Fi network. Otherwise you won't be able to connect.

To conclude, WPA2 encryption combined with a really strong password and MAC Address filtering is the best way to protect your Wi-Fi network from unauthorized access.

Stay safe when connecting to public networks

Now you know how to protect your home network, which means that you should be pretty safe when using Wi-Fi at home. But what about public Wi-Fi networks? Everybody loves using them and only too often we forget that these networks are unprotected and they are a huge safety hazard unless you take certain precautions.

The first thing you need to do when you are using a public network is tell Windows that it's public and potentially insecure. Most of the times Windows will ask you to specify network type when you connect to it for the first time. In case it doesn't, go to the **Control Panel**, click on **Network and Internet** and then go to **Network and Sharing Center**. Set your current network to **Public**.

While you are at it, I also recommend clicking on **Change advanced sharing settings**, opening the **Public profile** and turning off all sharing options. This will make sure that your computer doesn't allow anyone to connect to it remotely.

The next thing you should do is enable your firewall and make sure your anti-virus is active and up to date. The firewall is your first line of protection against intrusion and your anti-virus will protect you against malware. To enable your firewall in Windows 7, go to the **Control Panel - System and Security** - **Windows Firewall** - **Turn Windows Firewall on or off**. Also don't forget to configure your firewall to notify you when it blocks something:

To enable a firewall on a Mac, open **System Preferences** and select **Security**. Then choose **Firewall** and click on the little padlock at the bottom of the screen to enter your username and password, so that you can make the changes. Click on **Start** to enable the firewall.

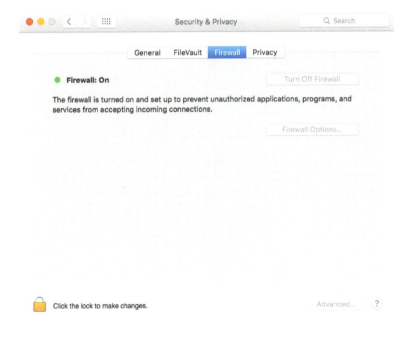

Now you can click on **Advanced…** and configure the firewall settings. Check the **Automatically allow signed software to receive incoming connections** checkbox, so that your Mac applications will be able to communicate with the rest of the world without you having to approve them every single time.

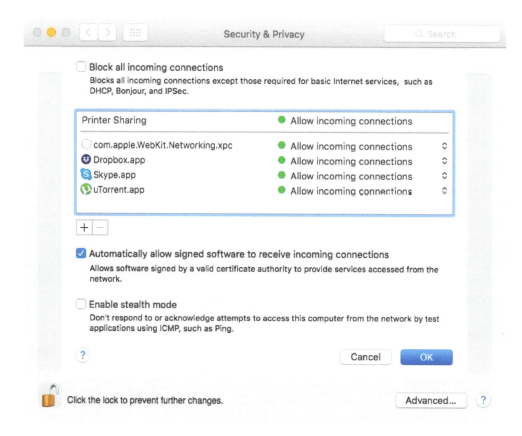

And last but not least, you can always use a free VPN (Virtual Private Network) to protect your identity. Instead of connecting to the Internet directly, you will establish an encrypted connection with a server, which will then connect you to the Internet. There are several free VPN services you can check out, such as VyprVPN, CyberGhost and ProXPN.

Now your network is secure. But let me tell you that no password will protect you if your system gets infected with malware designed to steal your personal information.

The first thing you should do is learn everything you can about the enemy. Only that way will you be able to protect yourself. So, let's move on to the next chapter and find out about viruses, malware and Trojans.

Know Your Enemy

Malware, Viruses, Trojans, Worms and Rootkits

As I've already told you in the first chapter of this book, there are countless security threats that you need to watch out for. Your computer can get infected in a lot of different ways, but the most common way to catch a virus or get a piece of malware installed on your system is to get infected when you are browsing the Web and downloading files. If you like to visit new websites, if you click on ads, and if you like downloading software, movies, music and ebooks from the Internet, then you can easily be infected with several pieces of malware that can cause a lot of damage.

Of course, there are ways you can protect yourself and even avoid getting infected in the first place. The first thing you need to remember is that different malware operates differently. So, to protect yourself from them, you need to know how different security threats work and how they affect your system.

First of all let's learn about malware, viruses, Trojans, worms and rootkits.

Malware

Malware is short for malicious software that is designed to compromise computers. For example, malware can disrupt or deny operations, collect the user's private information for identity theft purposes, gain unauthorized access to various system components, and behave in an abusive manner.

Basically, malware is a general term used by professionals to describe malicious, intrusive and hostile software or code.

A program is considered to be malware when its behavior and the intent of its creator are malicious. Malware includes computer viruses, worms, Trojan horses, spyware, adware, most rootkits and other malicious software. Malware is often used for Internet crime purposes and is fought by operating system and third party software developers, as well as by governments, businesses and pretty much everyone else.

Computer virus

Computer viruses are the most well-known security threat. A virus is a small piece of software that is written with the purpose to alter your computer settings and change the way your computer operates. Viruses do that without the user's knowledge or permission. Just like human viruses, computer viruses replicate themselves and spread to other computers, wrecking your computer in the process. However, some viruses do nothing but replicate themselves. There are two major types of viruses – resident and non-resident.

Viruses need to be able to execute a code and write to memory. That's why most viruses are attached to executable files, which are usually part of legitimate programs. When the user launches an infected program, the virus code gets executed at the same time.

When viruses are executed, they start searching for opportunities to replicate themselves. Resident viruses don't start searching for the host immediately, but rather load themselves in the memory and assign control to the host program. They then run in the background with the user none the wiser and infect new files when they are accessed by the host program.

Non-resident viruses behave in a different way. As soon as they are executed, they start looking for other things they can infect. When they find and infect new targets, they finally give control to the application they infected.

Viruses are often confused with other types of malware, such as Trojans, worms, rootkits, spyware and other infections.

Trojans

Just like the Trojan horse from Greek mythology, computer Trojan horses get inside your system and perform destructive actions. Unlike viruses, they don't replicate themselves. This doesn't mean that they are less dangerous. In fact, they can do more damage than viruses because most Trojan horses install themselves on your computer and grant remote access to your system to the hacker.
Once the Trojan is installed, the hacker can do everything your user account has privileges to do. Usually hackers use Trojan horses to:

- Steal your passwords and bank details
- Use your computer as part of a botnet
- Modify or delete files
- Log your keystrokes and watch your screen

To do all these things, Trojans need to communicate with the hacker and receive instructions.

The latest Trojan horses exploit a security flaw in old versions of Microsoft Internet Explorer and Google Chrome to use the infected computer as an anonymizer proxy to hide Internet usage in the most effective way. This allows the hacker to anonymously browse various sites, while all the tracking cookies are saved on the infected computer, and its IP address and history are logged. This allows hackers to completely cover their tracks.

Trojans are becoming more and more common, as botnets are becoming more popular among hackers.

Computer worms

Worms are one of the most dangerous pieces of malware. They use the network to copy themselves to other computers and they do so without the user's knowledge. Unlike viruses, worms don't need to be attached to another program, which makes them more dangerous than viruses. Worms consume bandwidth, can damage network and even completely wreck your PC.

There are different types of worms. Some of them do nothing but replicate themselves without causing any harm. However, other worms are designed to cause harm – they delete files on the host computer, install backdoors and other malware, or even turn the computer into a zombie that will do what the hacker wants as soon as it receives a command from the hacker or the worm. Some of the most well-known worms are the Sasser Worm, Win32 Conficker Worm and Mydoom.

It's not easy to protect yourself against worms, as worms exploit system vulnerabilities. The only way to stay relatively safe is to keep your operating system, your anti-virus and other software fully patched, and use a firewall.

Rootkits

Rootkits are little programs that are very difficult to detect - even the best anti-viruses can miss them. Rootkits infect various system components, but most of the time they target the kernel, firmware and user applications.

Rootkits hide themselves and grant the hacker continued privileged access to the system by circumventing user authentication. If your computer is infected with a rootkit, the hacker can do pretty much everything the computer administrator can with you not suspecting a thing.

Rootkits are difficult to detect because they are able to subvert the security software that is designed to find them. That's why quite often detecting rootkits requires the user to use alternative methods, such as behavioral methods, difference scanning, signature scans, memory dump analysis and using an alternative operating system to find the rootkit. Rootkits are not only difficult to detect, but also next to impossible to remove. That's especially true when the rootkit infects the kernel. When that's the case, the only option is to reinstall the operating system.

Now you know what these infections are and what they can do to your system. But there are other computer infections that are designed for the sole purpose of stealing your private data. We'll talk about them in the next chapter.

Beware of the Spies

Spyware and Keyloggers

You already know about malware, viruses and other malicious programs that get installed on your system with the main purpose of ruining it. But there are other types of malicious software. These programs don't ruin your PC as such and are pretty hard to detect. However, they often prove to be more dangerous than the traditional viruses because of the consequences of their operation. I'm talking about malware that spies on you and sends your private information to its master, the hacker. While getting rid of nasty viruses sometimes means that you have to reformat your hard drive, various forms of spyware can wreck your life, which can't be reformatted. That's because spyware infections are designed to steal your private data, so that the hacker can clear your bank account or even steal your identity. That's why spyware is so dangerous – it can land you in a mess that may take ages to sort out.

There are different types of spying software and you should know how spyware can steal your private data. In this chapter we are going to learn about the most common spying programs that hackers use – spyware and keyloggers.

Spyware

Basically, spyware are little programs that transmit your personal information to a hacker via Internet connection without your knowledge.

Spyware programs usually hide themselves from the user and make it difficult for basic anti-virus software to detect them. In most cases spyware gets installed without the user's consent together with other programs or as small add-ons you can't opt out of.

However, sometimes spyware gets installed by the user simply because the user doesn't have the patience to read EULAs (End User License Agreements) for the software he or she downloads from the Internet. Quite often the EULA actually mentions spyware, so when you click the "I Agree" button, you give your consent to install the spyware. When that's the case, there is nothing you can do legally to the software developer that infected you with spyware.

Most spyware programs are illegal. However, there are legitimate uses of spyware, especially keyloggers (software that logs keystrokes) when it gets installed on a corporate or public network for monitoring purposes.

Spyware is really dangerous because it's used by malicious persons to steal the user's personal information, such as passwords, credit card data and bank account details. In most cases, spyware is used to commit online identity theft. That's why spyware is also called privacy invasive software.

Even though spyware is difficult to detect by basic anti-virus programs, there is a lot of comprehensive anti-spyware programs available today. Spyware protection is an essential element of computer security.

Another, less dangerous type of spyware, are tracking cookies. They are often used by various websites to make your browsing more convenient by allowing you to stay logged in and recognizing you.
Tracking cookies are also used by advertisers to keep track of your browsing preferences and show you the most relevant ads. Most of the time there is no real harm in tracking cookies. But if you feel uncomfortable of someone tracking your browsing habits, you can always use the Private Browsing (Incognito) mode to delete cookies when the browser is closed and notify the advertisers that you don't want to be tracked.

Using the Private mode in Firefox

If you use Firefox, then it's easy to avoid being tracked – all you need to do is enable the Private Browsing mode. Here is how:

1.   Open **Firefox**, click on File and select **New Private Windows**. Alternatively press **Ctrl+Shift+P** on your keyboard

(Command+Shift+P on a Mac)

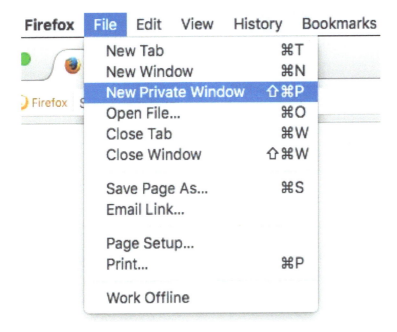

2.   You will get a message saying that your open tabs will be closed and saved for later, when you are finished with private browsing

3.   Click on the **Start Private Browsing** button and a private browsing session will begin

You can also notify advertisers that you don't want to be tracked by them. To do that, do the following:

1.   Open **Firefox** and type **about:preferences** in the address bar

2.   In the window that opens, click on the **Privacy** icon

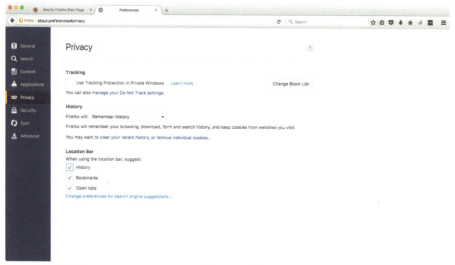

3.   Click on **manage your Do Not Track settings** and check the checkbox

4.   Click **OK** to save the changes

Using the Incognito mode in Google Chrome

Google Chrome has an option for you to browse the Web privately too. Here is how you can enable it:

1.   Open **Chrome** and click on the **Settings icon** ≡
2.   Select **New Incognito Window**. Alternatively press **Ctrl+Shift+N** on your keyboard (⌘-Shift-N on a Mac)

3.   A new window will open and you will be notified that you've gone incognito

4.   Type the URL of the website you want to visit in the address bar and start browsing the Web

Please note that using Private Browsing in Firefox or the Incognito mode in Chrome doesn't prevent websites from collecting your personal information and does not protect you from spyware, malware, or keyloggers. What it does is merely instruct the browser not to record history and delete cookies when you close all Private Browsing or Incognito windows.

Keyloggers

A keylogger is a program that logs every single keystroke on the keyboard performed by the user. And that's done without the user's knowledge. The logs can be viewed by the owner of the keylogging software. This means that everything you type, including all your passwords to all your online banking accounts, becomes available to a third party. Just imagine how disastrous that can be!

Even though this is controversial, there are also legitimate uses of keylogging software. For example, keylogger applications are often used for parental control purposes, by schools, offices and even FBI. For example, in 2000, the FBI captured the usernames and passwords of two suspected Russian cybercriminals using a keylogger that was covertly installed on a system the criminals used to access their computers back in Russia. With the help of this keylogger the FBI was able to access the suspects' computers and obtain the necessary evidence to prosecute them.

Legitimate keyloggers can be both software and hardware keyloggers. Most of the time illegal keyloggers are software programs that get installed on an unsuspecting user's computer in exchange for free smileys, screensavers and similar junk.

Now you know about the main types of infections that are created specifically for the Windows operating system. But why is Windows so insecure? Read on to find out.

A Window for Infections

Why Windows Has More Viruses than Other Operating Systems

Everybody knows that Windows is the most insecure of all the operating systems. Malware just loves it. But why is that? Of course, Windows is the most popular operating system and that's partly the reason why malware developers love it, but it's not the only one. You see, the decisions made by Microsoft in the past made the OS a fertile ground for all sorts of malicious software. It got to the point that every single Windows user needs an anti-virus, whereas Linux users are perfectly safe without it.

So, how did we, Windows users, get there? Let's have a look at the reasons.

Windows is popular

This is the number one reason why malware developers invest their time into creating malware for Windows. The vast majority of the world's desktops and laptops use Windows and nearly all businesses run on Windows (I've never heard of a company that has Linux on all of its office computers). So if a malware developer wants to write a keylogger to steal important information from average users or businesses, Windows is the best choice. After all, that's where most users are.

As you can see, popularity can be a security bane. Compare Windows to film stars and you'll understand. Both need to hire security (an anti-virus in case of Windows). But being popular is not the only reason why Windows is a favorite target.

Windows was not designed for security

Historically, Windows was not built with security in mind, whereas Linux and Mac OS X (based on Unix) were created from the start as multi-user operating systems (systems that allow people to log in with limited user accounts). But the original Windows never was such a system.

Some of you may remember the days of DOS. Well, DOS was a single-user operating system and Windows was built on top of that. I mean, back in those times everyone thought that Windows 3.1, 95, 98, and Me were really advanced, but in fact they were operating on top of DOS. The good old single-user DOS. So there were no user accounts, no file permissions and no security restrictions. But then Windows NT appeared.

Windows NT is the core of all Windows version from Windows 2000. Even Windows 8 uses it. Windows NT has everything that is needed for essential security, which includes the ability to have restricted user accounts and permissions. The only problem is that Microsoft was kind of late with designing consumer versions of Windows with the necessary security features. The first one was Windows XP SP2.

The original XP supported multiple user accounts with limited privileges, but nobody really used them. People simply logged into their Windows XP systems using the Administrator account.

One of the reasons for that was that it was really convenient to use the autologin feature. But there was another reason - a lot of software didn't work unless the user was logged in as Administrator. Add to that the fact that Windows XP didn't have a built-in anti-virus and you'll understand why it became an easy target for all sorts of threats. Basically, an unpatched Windows XP system was infected by worms like Blaster within minutes of connecting directly to the Internet.

Another huge security hole was Windows XP's autorun feature that automatically ran programs from any media device connected to a computer. This was the perfect way for criminals to install rootkits. Usually a criminal would leave an infected USB drive or CD disc somewhere where an employee of a company they were targeting was sure to pick it up. As soon as the drive was plugged in, malware would install itself on the computer. And since most computers were used with administrative privileges, the malware would have complete access to everything.

As you can see, Microsoft didn't really make Windows XP bulletproof and it was not a system that could survive the dangers of the Internet.

Software downloads

In many ways, Windows is more dangerous than mobile operating systems like Android. While Android users and Linux desktop users can download software that is not listed on Google Play or Linux software repositories, most people don't do that and download stuff from trusted developers.
And Apple is even more vigilant when it comes to third-party downloads. But with Windows you can download and install any program you find on the Web. In a way, it's cool. But it's also really dangerous and a lot of less experienced users download and install dangerous files. The most common are screensavers, fake anti-virus programs and bogus registry cleaners.

Microsoft realized that operating systems with a trusted source of software downloads is the way to go and created the Windows Store for app downloads when they released Windows 8. It's a shame that they didn't create something similar for desktop applications.

What was done to improve security

Thankfully, Microsoft hasn't been idle and did at least something to fix Windows security holes. Their first step was issuing Windows XP Service Pack 2, which included a better firewall and several other security features like a security center that urges users to install an anti-virus program.

Windows Vista went even further and introduced User Account Control - a feature that finally encouraged people to use limited user accounts. Today, Windows uses limited user accounts by default, has a built-in firewall that is enabled by default, and no longer automatically runs *.exe files. And Windows 8 and 10 even come with a built-in anti-virus, which is rather good. Windows is still the least secure operating system, but it's getting better.

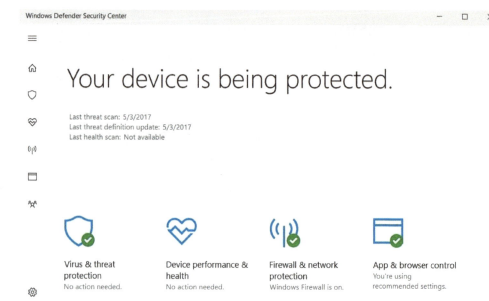

As you can see, there isn't a sole reason why Windows has the most viruses - it is a combination of factors. The fact that Windows is so popular adds to it, but Microsoft is also responsible for not introducing the necessary security features in time.

Even with the security improvements made in Windows 8, the less savvy desktop user is still in danger of infecting the system with software downloads and missing the warning signs of malware.

But what about Mac OS? Are there any infections that affect it in the same way they affect Windows? I'll tell you about them in the next chapter.

Do Apples Get Worms?

An Overview of Mac Infections

One of the reasons why people switch from Windows to Mac is because they think that there is no Mac malware. Every time you read comments to computer security-related blog posts, you see someone saying something like "The easiest way to avoid viruses is to switch to Mac". Well, I only wish it were this way. Unfortunately, even the best apples get an occasional worm (sorry, couldn't resist the pun!). There are Mac viruses and there is Mac malware out there, so even Mac users can't be 100% sure that they won't get infected.

There is a common misconception that Macs don't have any security flaws. However, now even Apple stopped boasting that OS X "doesn't get PC viruses" after a couple of widespread Mac infections in 2012. Yes, Mac is still a lot safer than Windows and, unlike Windows, doesn't have mass security holes. However, some of its components are not particularly safe and have various vulnerabilities.

One example of a Mac component with various security flaws is the Safari Web browser. It has a bad reputation among security specialists, as there are exploits that can be found and used even by amateurs.

The good news is that Mac OS X is pretty good at catching viruses without the help of any third party security software. There is a feature called File Quarantine, which was first introduced in Leopard and made its way to newer Mac OS X versions. This feature works in a very simple, yet effective way.

Basically, when you download a suspicious file using either Safari or Mail, the file will be quarantined and scanned for Trojans using what Apple calls XProtect. Just like anti-malware programs for Windows, XProtect uses daily updated malware definitions to identify malicious programs.

So, if the downloaded file is a Trojan and you try to open it, you will get a warning message from the OS telling you that the application is malware. As you can see, Mac OS X comes with built-in security software. A very efficient way of protecting Mac users, if you ask me.

How does malware get installed on a Mac?

Most Apple applications support quarantine, so you should be protected even if you use third-party software. However, some peer-to-peer sharing programs avoid the quarantine feature and put you at risk. Most Mac infections get installed on from torrent and illegal download sites, so it's best to avoid these sites altogether.

Another way Macs get infected is when the user actually installs the malware on the system. A lot of Mac malware has adapted the technique popular among Windows viruses when malware is masquerading as legitimate software. For example, the user thinks that he or she is downloading an HD video player or a codec, but in reality it's malware pretending to be something else. That's why you should never disable XProtect (even if its warnings seem annoying) and you should never download any software from unknown websites. There are plenty of legitimate software download websites where all programs are tested for infections. CNET Download.com is the most popular of them all and has an excellent Mac category.

Mac infections of the past

If you think that Macs never got infected in the past, then you are wrong. Here is a list of the most famous Mac infections of the previous years.

OSX/Leap-A / OSX.Oomp

This worm appeared in 2006 and used to spread itself through instant messaging via iChat. Its targets were Power-PC based systems running Mac OS X. The worm file, latestpics.tgz, pretended to be a JPEG image and sent itself to everybody on the user's buddy list. As soon as the recipient opened the file, his or her Mac became infected.

AppleScript.THT

This is a Trojan that appeared in 2008. It disabled security software, stole passwords and even managed to take the users' pictures using MacBook's or iMac's built-in camera. And it could take screenshots of your desktop.

This Trojan had been distributed in the form of a game or a utility. When installed, it exploited the Remote Desktop Agent feature of Mac OS X Tiger and Leopard. Basically, this Trojan allowed its owner to take total control over your Mac. Not nice.

OSX.Iservice and OSX.Iservice.B (iBotNet)

These Mac infections first appeared in 2009. They were embedded in illegal pirated copies of iWork '09 and Adobe PhotoShop CS4. The infected software was usually shared on popular torrent websites. The OSX.Iservice.B was the first Mac infection that attempted to create a Mac botnet with the purpose of launching denial-of-service attacks.

Koobface or Boonana

This piece of Mac malware appeared in 2010. It was a Java applet that appeared on Facebook and Twitter, and was already well-known by Windows users. What it did was trick unsuspected users into clicking on a link to a video, saying something like "Is this you in this video?".

Luckily, the malware was too buggy to work correctly, but it's still around so be careful and don't click on any suspicious links unless you want to be infected with a nasty Trojan.

Flashback

Flashback was a Mac Trojan that acted like a bucket of cold water for unsuspecting 600,000+ Mac users in April 2012. When this infection hit, it became obvious that even though Macs are more secure than Windows PCs, they stayed this way simply because malware manufacturers didn't really give them a lot of attention. But as Mac market share grows, it's starting to become a target.

Anyway, what exactly is Flashback? Flashback is a piece of malware that was designed to record passwords and other user information from their browsers. In addition to that, it managed to steal user information from apps like Skype. The malware installs code that collects personal information and then sends it to its owner.

The malware is called Flashback because it presents itself as an Adobe Flash installer, which is how it managed to infect so many Macs. Users didn't suspect a thing and thought that they were installing a legitimate browser plugin. Then Flashback got even worse because it didn't require any user interaction to get installed.

You may be asking yourself why Flashback managed to infect so many Macs. Well, sad as it is, it's largely Apple's fault. You see, Apple doesn't ship Adobe Flash on its computers, which means that users need to download Flash separately. But that's not all. Apple doesn't use Java public releases. Instead, it creates and maintains its own versions. Unfortunately, Flashback utilized a fault in Java that was fixed by Java ages ago, but which was neglected by Apple staff.

Apple has taken the necessary measures to protect Macs from several versions of Flashback. But not all of them can be detected by XProtect because they use Java to execute their files. Luckily, you can always check if you have Flashback or not using F-Secure Flashback detection and removal software or a tool from Symantec.

A hacker attack on Apple employees

This was the most recent Mac infection. It happened in February 2013 and affected Apple employees. There isn't a lot of information about this attack, but it has been revealed that only a small number of systems got affected and there was no evidence that any data was stolen.

Nevertheless, it's alarming that even Apple's internal computers are vulnerable and can be infected through developer websites. Clearly, as more people use Macs, more malware developers start working on Mac viruses.

Mac anti-virus software

As you can see, a Mac anti-virus is not such a bad idea after all, especially now that Macs are becoming a target for hackers. Even though Macs are still a lot more secure than Windows PCs, it's wise to install an anti-virus.

Specialists from the leading security companies like Sophos and McAfee recommend installing an anti-virus on your Mac to make sure that no infections can seep through. All right, if you are a home Mac user, you can get away with just being careful when installing stuff and browsing the Web. But if there is more than your photos and emails at stake (I'm talking about things like your company's confidential information), then you do need an anti-virus. Here are scenarios when you absolutely need to install Mac security software:

• You are using a Mac in a corporate environment

• You are a freelancer and store your clients' billing information on your Mac

• You download everything and anything without checking it first

• You share a lot of files and don't want to be accused of spreading viruses

• You are a novice Mac user and don't know what's what

Remember that even though right now Mac infections are not as common as viruses for Windows, the Flashback incident showed that Apple computers are not as secure as they once were. As more and more people start using Apple's products, infections for Mac OS are becoming more common, more sophisticated, and more dangerous.

Right, now you know a lot about infections. So let's find out how you can avoid getting infected and protect yourself.

Protect Your Mac

Simple Tips to Improve Mac Security

As we've already discussed, Mac computers are not as secure as they used to be in the past. This means that you will need to pay a bit more attention to the security of your system and configure its settings in such a way that malware will have an even harder time getting in. Here are several simple things you can do to improve the security of your Mac.

Configure your preferences

OS X has a lot of preferences that will help you make your system more secure. The first one that is worth mentioning is FileVault - a preference that allows you to encrypt your data. FileVault has been available since Mac OS X 10.3, but was hugely improved with Lion. It no longer slows down your computer to any noticeable degree, and it doesn't cause any conflicts with Time Machine anymore, which makes backups a piece of cake.

Another useful security option is Application Sandboxing. This option limits what a program can do, like being able to open a file or access the network. This means that if one of your applications has a vulnerability, anyone accessing your Mac through it shouldn't be able to gain control of other parts of your computer.

And last but not least, there is Gatekeeper. This new System Preferences option is designed to make your Mac behave like an iOS device in terms of security - it lets you set it up to only allow apps purchased from the App Store to run on your Mac.

Gatekeeper has different security levels for you to choose from. If you want to, you can allow apps from "identified developers" who aren't on the Mac App Store (Apple is currently creating a list of them). Or if you are not really bothered about system security and have an I-install-whatever-I-want attitude, you can switch Gatekeeper to the lowest security mode, which is basically what we've been used to since the early days of computing.

Create a separate user account

Just like with Windows, you can boost your Mac's security level by simply creating a separate, non-admin user account for everyday activity and only use the default administrative one when you really need to.

To create a standard user account, go to **System Preferences** and then go to the **Accounts** pane. Create a **Standard** user account and use it for things like browsing the Web, checking email, and so on.

Using a non-admin account will protect you against zero-day threats because they will not be able to do the full amount of damage without administrative privileges.

Get rid of Adobe Flash

Sad as it is, Adobe's products are long-time favorite malware attractors. And the recent Flashback attack only confirmed that. So, if you don't want hackers to take full control over your Mac, it's best to uninstall Flash altogether. Use Adobe's special uninstall tools to do this.

If you do need to use Flash and don't want to uninstall it from your Mac, keep it as up-to-date as possible. Make a habit of visiting Adobe's website and checking for Flash updates.

Use a secure Web browser

Since Apple computers don't come with built-in Flash, uninstalling Flash Player will mean that you will need to use a browser that has built-in flash if you still want to be able to access flash content. The only browser that has built-in flash is Google Chrome. Switching to Chrome makes a lot of sense from the security point of view because Google keeps it updated regularly and the updates are automatic.

Uninstall Java

Java is another favorite malware target. If you don't use applications that rely on Java, it's best that you completely uninstall it from your Mac. This especially makes sense because Apple doesn't allow you to get updates directly from Oracle and often forgets to patch it in time. This means that when it comes to Java, your Mac is less secure than Windows PCs, which get timely updates.

To get rid of Java, go to **Applications - Utilities** and uncheck the boxes next to all Java versions listed there. Alternatively, open your browser, go to **Preferences** and uncheck all checkboxes related to Java.

Use Keychain to manage your passwords

Good news for Mac users is that your OS comes with a built-in password manager - Keychain. This tool can help you protect yourself from phishing attacks and always use strong, unique passwords for each of your online accounts. Keychain will store all your passwords and other confidential information, such as certificates, in a secure way. You can enable Keychain under **Applications - Utilities**.

Disable IPv6, Bluetooth and AirPort

Connectivity ports are also loved by hackers because they make easy entry points to your system. Disabling them will make your system more secure. IPv6 is not yet commonly used, which means that you can safely disable it. To do that, follow these steps:

1.   Select **Apple** menu, go to **System Preferences** and then click **Network**

2.   If **Network Preferences** are locked, click on the lock and enter administrative password

3.   Now select the network service you want to use with IPv6 like Ethernet or AirPort

4.   Now click **Advanced** and then click **TCP/IP**

5.   Select **Off** under **Configure IPv6**

And if you are not using Bluetooth or AirPort, it's a good idea to disable them too. This will make your Mac more secure and you can always re-enable them whenever you need to.

Update your Mac regularly

Most attacks on Mac take advantage of faults in outdated programs. Commonly exploited programs are Adobe Reader, Microsoft Office, but other outdated applications are a potential threat as well. That's why it's really important to make sure your software and your operating system are always up to date. So, whenever you see **Software Update's** prompt, act fast and install the updates. These updates are there for a reason and they'll make your Mac more secure.

Don't forget to reboot your Mac whenever prompted without leaving it too long.

Install Little Snitch

Your firewall will most likely stop things that are trying to break into your computer. But what if something is making your information leak out?

There is an app that will help you spot and stop that. It's called **Little Snitch**. You can tell the app to trust specific applications, so that it won't bother you every time you connect to iTunes. But it will be sure to spot any activity by an unknown or untrusted app. This will draw your attention to potential offenders and act quickly if needed. Little Snitch has a lot of privacy options, so make sure you check them all out.

Your Mac should be a lot more secure now, especially if you've installed a Mac security suite.

Hope Is Good, Prevention Is Better

How to Avoid Getting Infected

Modern anti-malware software is pretty advanced and can delete most infections. Some programs even have the capability to delete rootkits, which are the worst type of malware and are very difficult to remove. However, you should not fully rely on your anti-virus program and think that it will save you from all infections. Because it won't. Even the best security programs occasionally miss malware and viruses, especially new threats. To tell you the truth, fully relying on your anti-virus to deal with infections is the surest way to get infected with something nasty and eventually have to reinstall your operating system. That's why you should do everything to avoid getting infected in the first place. Here are some guidelines for you to follow.

Use quality security software

Now, every Windows user knows that one should have anti-virus software. In fact, computer manufacturers know it too and they install trial versions of products like McAfee and Norton on their laptops. And that's why a lot of users don't bother getting a new anti-virus. You see, quite a few people think that the trial version they have installed provides good protection.
Worse still, a lot of people don't renew their subscription even when the trial expires because they think that they are still protected. And that's the ideal conditions to get infected – viruses and malware evolve constantly and an outdated anti-virus is no good at all. That's why you should either purchase a subscription or uninstall the pre-installed trial and get different security software.

When choosing security software, keep in mind two main factors – detection rates and effect on system performance. A good anti-virus should have a high independent rating and shouldn't consume too much system resources. Otherwise you could stay relatively unprotected and your computer could become slow.

A good place to check independent security software ratings is AV Comparatives (http://www.av-comparatives.org). As for the software's effect on system performance, you should read independent reviews by industry experts from CNET, PC World and other computer publications.

Another thing you should consider is the price. Anti-virus software is quite costly and Internet security software is even more expensive. Luckily, there are free security programs such as Microsoft Security Essentials, which are very good too.

Keep your anti-virus up to date

One thing you should never fail to do is keep your security software up to date. An outdated anti-virus is no better than having no anti-virus at all because it can't detect anything. That's why you should ensure that your anti-virus is configured to update itself automatically whenever new definitions are released. This way you will always stay protected.

Automatic updates should be enabled by default. If they are not enabled, you should go to program settings and enable automatic updates.

Scan your PC regularly

Performing regular scans with anti-virus and anti-malware software is something we all know we should do, but often neglect. And that's wrong because regular scans can help you nip infections in the bud.

One of the reasons why people neglect regular scans is because the default scheduled time for them is almost always something ridiculous, like 3 a.m. Don't know about you, but I'm usually asleep at that time of night and my computer is switched off. That's why I always recommend changing the scheduled scan time to a time when your computer is on, but you are not using it. Lunchtime is the ideal time for me. So, let's configure your anti-virus schedule. I'll use Microsoft Security Essentials as an example, but configuring a different anti-virus is similar enough.

1.   Open your anti-virus program and go to **Setting**

2.   Locate the item that refers to scheduled scans and make sure they are enabled

3.   Select **Quick scan** or **Full scan**, and choose the time that suits you best

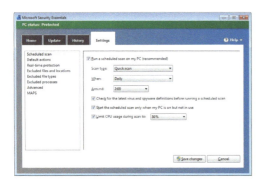

4.   Select additional options, such as reduced CPU load or the option to start the scan only when the computer is not in use

☑ Start the scheduled scan only when my PC is on but not in use

5.   Click on **Save changes** (or **OK**, depending on your anti-virus) and you're done.

Use your common sense

This may sound funny, but your best protector from viruses, malware, phishing scams and online fraud is your common sense. So use it when you are browsing the Web, downloading software, music and movies, and doing your shopping online.

The first thing you should remember is to never click any links on suspicious websites. If a website looks low quality, is stuffed with advertisements, displays porn ads and annoys you with pop-up windows, leave it immediately without clicking on anything. It also won't hurt to scan your computer with security software after visiting suspicious websites.

Another thing you should check and double-check is downloads. No matter whether you download eBooks, software, videos or MP3s, you can get infected through these files and by the download websites, especially if they are torrent sites. So, every time you download something from the Web, check the downloaded file with your anti-virus and anti-malware programs before opening it. This is especially true for ZIP and RAR archives, as well as PDF files.

And last but not least, never click on any links in suspicious emails and never open any attachments without scanning them with your security software first. You should especially avoid the emails in your Spam or Junk folder. In fact, don't even open unsolicited email, as most of the time it contains spam, is designed to trick you and may have infected attachments.

Sometimes you might receive suspicious-looking emails from friends. These emails are likely to have links in them saying that you should check out something cool. If that happens, don't click on any links and contact your friends immediately, notifying them of the suspicious emails. Chances are that their account got hacked and their computer got configured to send viruses and spam to everyone on their contact list.

Disable Remote Desktop and Remote Assistance services

If you are a home user, then Windows runs a lot of services that you will never need. Most of them are geared towards office workers or people with their own network.
Most of these services are harmless, but some of them have the potential to let malware through and grant hackers access to your system.
Naturally, Microsoft never intended these services to be used maliciously, but they often get abused.

Remote Desktop and **Remote Assistance** services are potentially the most vulnerable points in Microsoft Windows XP. In Windows, 7 Microsoft recognized the flaw and by default Remote Desktop is disabled. However, if you are still using Windows XP, you should disable Remote Assistance and Remote Desktop unless your computer is part of a network and requires system administrators to be able to access it remotely. Here is how you can disable Remote Desktop and Remote Assistance:

1.   Click on **Start** and go to **Control Panel**

2.   Go to **Performance and Maintenance** and double-click the **System** icon

3.   Select the **Remote** tab

4.   Uncheck **Allow Remote Assistance invitations to be sent from this computer**

5.   In the same tab click **Advanced**

6.   Uncheck **Allow users to connect remotely to this computer**

7.   Click **Apply**, then click **OK**

Now hackers won't be able to gain easy access to your system. And don't worry, your Internet connection and programs that use the Internet will work perfectly well with these services disabled.

Now you know how you can avoid getting infected. But there is more you can do to keep your computer safe. Let's find out how PC maintenance can make your Windows more secure.

Keep Your PC in Top Shape

Computer Maintenance Can Help Prevent and Remove Infections

In the previous chapters of this book we've been discussing computer threats, various forms of malware, and concentrated on some ways you can protect your computer from becoming infected. But now let's talk about PC maintenance. You might ask why talk about computer maintenance in a book that is focused on computer security. Well, simply because regular computer cleanup can help you avoid infections, keep your system more secure and even delete traces of old Trojans and viruses.

When you browse the Web, download videos, software, music, enter your passwords, and so on, all this information gets recorded in history files, temporary Internet files, and cookies. As you already know, it's only too easy to access the information stored on your hard drive, especially if your computer gets infected. In fact, a lot of infections reside in browser temporary folders and work hard transmitting information about the websites you visit. This information is then shared with advertisers. Ever wondered why you are getting tons of spam and various pop-ups keep appearing? Well, that can be because a piece of spyware is sitting in your temporary Internet files.

When you perform disk cleanup, history files, temporary files and browser cookies get deleted along with other junk files. Junk files accumulate over time and only serve a particular purpose when they are in use. As soon as the task for which the temporary files were created is done, they are not needed anymore. However, most temporary files are kept for a lot longer than necessary, sometimes for months. This has a lot of disadvantages.

The main disadvantage of having your computer cluttered with junk files is their negative effect on system performance. Junk files are the most common cause of computer slow-downs and they can also consume a lot of disk space. That's why you should run disk cleanup every once in a while, ideally at least once a month.

But there is another reason why you should pay attention to disk cleanup and that's security. After all, why would anyone want to store files that tell everything about their browsing habits and sometimes even store passwords?

Delete Temporary Internet Files

If you want to quickly delete Temporary Internet Files and free up some disk space, clearing your browser's cache is the way to go. This will delete files like history traces and cookies, and thus make your browser more secure. You can delete Temporary Internet Files right from your browser:

Internet Explorer 8 or 9:

1.   Open Internet Explorer and press **Ctrl+Shift+Del**
2.   Check the relevant checkboxes. I recommend selecting **Temporary Internet Files**, **Cookies** and **History**

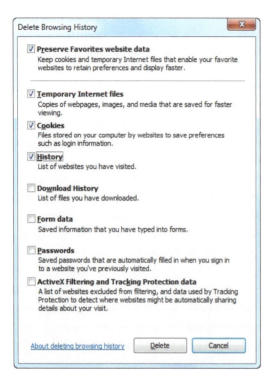

3.   Click on the **Delete** button

4.   Close the browser. Reboot your computer for good measure.

Firefox:

1.   Pressing **Ctrl+Shift+Del** will work here too

2.   Choose the time range and then click on the arrow next to **Details**

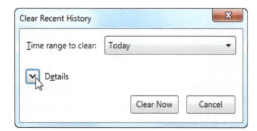

3.　　Select what you want to clean up. Like in Internet Explorer, I recommend deleting **Browsing & Download History**, **Cookies**, and **Cache**

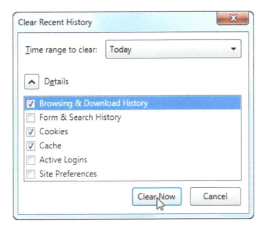

4.　　Click on **Clear Now**

Google Chrome:

1.　　Press **Ctrl+Shift+Del**
2.　　Check the relevant checkboxes and select the time period from the drop-down menu

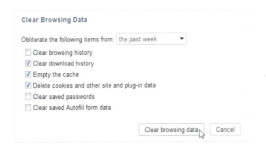

3.　　Select the relevant checkboxes
4.　　Click on **Clear Browsing Data**

Safari:

1.　　Open **Safari**, click on the **Safari** menu item and select **Clear History**

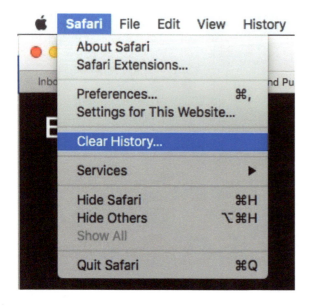

2.　　You will get a confirmation window where you can set the range and start the cleanup

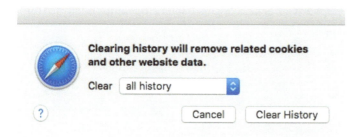

3.　　Now click on the **Safari** menu item again and select **Preferences**

4.   Click on the **Privacy** icon, then click on **Manage Website Data…**

5.   A new dialog box will open. Click on the **Remove All** button to remove all items or select the ones you want to delete and click on **Remove**

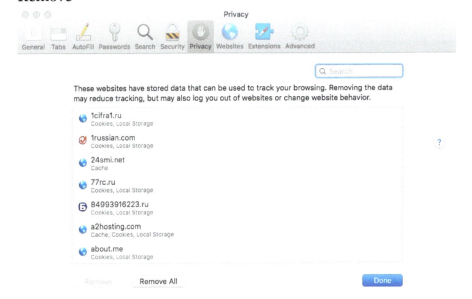

6.   Click **Done** to finish

Now Temporary Internet Files, cookies and history will be gone. But you can protect yourself even better and free up even more disk space by running disk cleanup.

Run disk cleanup

Like I said before, temporary files and history records can store private information like your passwords, email addresses, phone number, and sometimes even your credit card details. That's why deleting these files will help you make your system more secure. In addition to temporary files, there are system logs, memory dumps, contents of the prefetch folder and so on. All these files are a potential security threat and that's why you need to delete them on a regular basis. So, let's get the job done!

Windows XP:

1.   Click on **Start** and go to **Programs – Accessories – System Tools**
2.   Launch the **Disk Cleanup tool**
3.   Select the drive you want to clean up and let the program analyze it

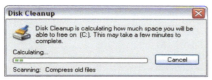

4.   Review the results and click **OK** to perform the cleanup

Windows 7:

1.   Click on **Start**, type **Disk Cleanup** into the search box

2.   Launch the **Disk Cleanup** tool. It will offer you to choose the drive you wish to clean up

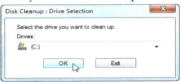

3.   Click **OK** and let the tool analyze your drive

4.   Now review the list of files to be deleted and click **OK**

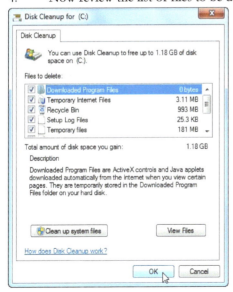

Windows 8 & 10:

1.   Open the **Charms bar** and click on **Search**

2.   In the search box, type in **Disk Cleanup** and click on **Settings**

3.   Click on **Free up disk space by deleting unnecessary files**.

This will open the Disk Cleanup tool

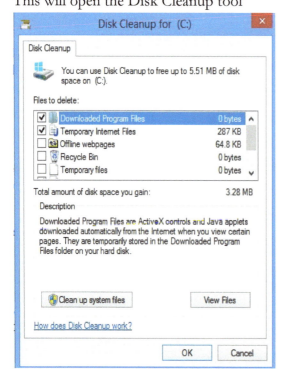

Now the majority of temporary files should be gone. However, Windows Disk Cleanup utility doesn't remove things like memory dumps and prefetch folder data. The information in either of them can potentially be used by malicious persons to gain access to your private records. That's why it's best to use a third party disk cleanup tool. There are plenty of utilities on the market, but I recommend FileCleaner Pro and CCleaner. They can delete a lot more junk files than the built-in Windows utility.

Mac users can clean up, speed up and protect their Macs with CleanMyMac or MacKeeper.

Optimize Windows

Another thing you should do on a regular basis is perform Windows optimization and maintain the registry. The registry is the central database of the Windows operating system. It stores all settings for every single bit of your computer - your hardware, software, user profiles and everything else.

Every time even the simplest action is performed on your computer, it gets recorded in the registry. You change your wallpaper and the registry gets updated. You configure a new homepage for your browser and the registry reflects the change. And if you install or uninstall a piece of software, hundreds of registry settings are modified. Without the registry your Windows won't work.

But I have some bad news for you. You see, the fact that the registry is the core database within Windows makes it very attractive to malware. That's why a lot of infections target the Windows registry, write themselves in its settings and then modify other registry settings to take full control of your computer.

When a piece of malware is detected and deleted by your security software, it can leave some traces behind, particularly in the Windows registry. This makes the removal incomplete and your computer stays infected even if your security software scans are coming all clear. But your computer can still be showing signs of infections, such as crashes, strange behavior and loss of speed. Registry optimization can help you delete traces of malware and make your computer as good as new.

There are plenty of Windows optimizers available for download. However, not all of them are reliable. You see, quite a few actually contain malware and can do more harm than good to your PC. That's why you should always ensure that the app of your choice is legitimate and virus-free.

It's pretty easy to check whether a system optimization program is safe or not. All you need to do is go to one of the legitimate software download sites, such as CNET Download.com or Softpedia.com, and read reviews for various registry cleaners. All software featured on these download sites is checked for infections by the site owners and user reviews should give you an idea of how effective the app is. Make sure you read the reviews well and don't let fake ratings affect your decision.

One of the system optimizers that I like for its effectiveness and ease of use is Easy PC Optimizer. It has a very intuitive interface, does a good job optimizing, cleaning and defragmenting Windows, and always backs up any changes made to your system.

Here is how you can optimize Windows with Easy PC Optimizer:

1.   Launch Easy PC Optimizer by double-clicking on its icon on your desktop

2.   Select the Windows categories you wish to scan (I recommend selecting all of them)

3.   Click on the Start Scan button to start the scan

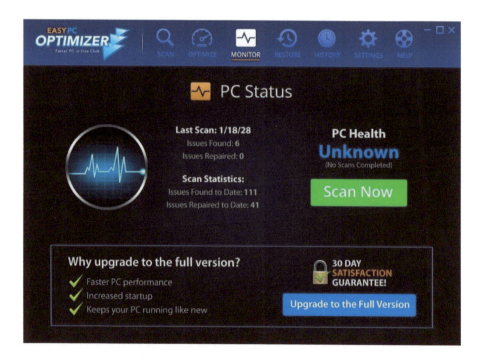

4.   Easy PC Optimizer will scan your computer

5.   Review results and click on Fix Errors

Easy PC Optimizer can do more than simply clean and optimize
Windows. It can also defragment the registry to free up RAM, clean junk
files and browser history, help you manage system startup, optimize your
Internet connection, manage large files and optimize Windows services.
All in all, this tool is worth having for everyone wanting to have a fast,
responsive and protected computer.

Now your system should be pretty secure. Nevertheless, you need to
know what to do when you get infected. In the next chapter, I'm going
to show you how to remove the most common infections.

Get Your Computer Disinfected

How to Remove the Most Common Viruses

Every single computer user dreads getting a virus that will wreak his or her PC. That's why we all invest in computer security software and do all we can to avoid getting infected. However, sometimes things go wrong and a piece of malware manages to install itself on your computer. And that's when you need to take action and remove the malware.

In most cases a scan with your anti-virus will detect the infection and the anti-virus will either remove it completely or place it in quarantine. However, in some cases malware infects your computer in such a way that your anti-virus won't detect it. And some infections, like fake anti-virus programs, simply disable your security software. So, what to do if your anti-virus can't deal with an infection? Here are some tips that should help.

General malware cleanup

If your anti-virus says that there are no infections, but you think your computer is infected with a piece of malware, you should get a second opinion. Now, I'm not telling you to call your friend and ask him or her to have a look at your PC. What I mean is that you should scan your computer with another anti-malware program.

Before we proceed, there is one thing you should know. Never-ever install two different anti-virus programs at the same time. Having more than one anti-viruses will not only fail to boost the security of your PC, but is likely to cause conflicts, system errors and crashes. However, you can have an anti-virus, an anti-malware and an anti-spyware installed at the same time.

So, the first thing you'll need to do is download an anti-malware program to scan your PC. I recommend using Malwarebytes' Anti-Malware – a free malware removal tool that is very effective when it comes to infections most popular anti-viruses miss.

Download it and install it on to your computer. After the installation is complete, allow Malwarebytes' to update its definitions.

When Malwarebytes' is installed on your PC, you will need to boot your computer in Safe Mode. Safe Mode is a special Windows boot mode, which loads only essential Windows drivers and setting.

So if a virus is locking files to protect itself, they will get unlocked when you boot into Safe Mode. To do that, reboot your computer and keep tapping **F8** when your computer screen is still black. A list of boot options will appear. Use the arrow keys to select **Safe Mode** and press **Enter**. Then select the operating system you wish to load. Log in as administrator.

Now open Malwarebytes' and run a full scan.

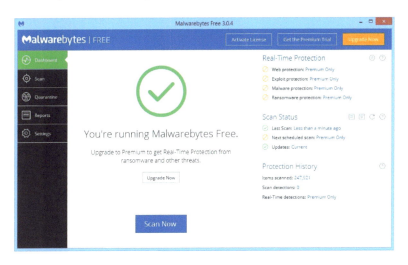

 This may take a while, but performing a full scan rather than a quick scan is really worth it, as it has a better chance to detect an infection your anti-virus might have missed. If anything is found, follow the prompts to remove the infection.

Now that all infections are deleted, reboot your computer. Keep tapping **F8** while the screen is still black, then use the arrow keys to select **Normal Mode** and press **Enter**.

In addition to Malwarebytes', you can scan your PC with anti-spyware solutions.

And now I'm going to provide some suggestions how to remove the most common PC infection – a Google redirect virus.

Removing Google redirect virus

A Google redirect virus is one of the most common infections today. This infection is a browser hijacker that hijacks your Google searches and redirects you to a particular site. Here is a scenario how Google redirect virus works:

You are searching Google for a bit of information. This can be something for college, a movie, a pizza recipe – anything at all. So, you get a bunch of search results from Google. You see the one that looks like the answer to your query and you click on it. But Google doesn't take you to the site listed in the search results. In fact, you are being taken to an entirely different website. No matter on which search result you click, you get the same website. In other words, you are being redirected by the Google redirect virus. Most of the time it's a site that asks you to enter some sort of personal information or tries to flog you a product.

The bad news is that the Google redirect virus is not just a simple hijacker – it's a complicated piece of malware that belongs to the rootkit family. That's why it's usually so difficult to remove. This particular rootkit belongs to the Rootkit.Win32.TDSS family. Luckily, top security software manufacturers like Kaspersky and Symantec have utilities that can assist you with the Google redirect virus removal.

So, if you are infected with the Google redirect virus, the first thing you should do is download **TDSSKiller.exe** from Kaspersky's website. If the rootkit is preventing you from downloading the file, try downloading it to a virus-free computer and transfer it to the infected PC using a USB flash drive.

Now that you have downloaded the TDSSKiller file, you'll need to execute it. Again, the rootkit might try to prevent you from running it. If that's the case, simply right-click on the TDSSKiller.exe icon and select **Rename**. Change the file name to something that doesn't look suspicious to the rootkit, for example daisy.com. Keep in mind that the new name needs to have the .com extension to work.

Now run the utility and click on the **Start scan** button.

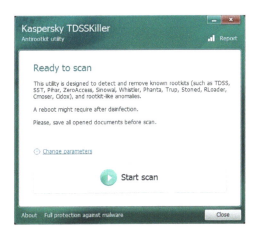

The tool will scan your computer for the TDSS rootkit.

Note that the tool scans your computer for both malicious and suspicious objects.

When the scan is finished, the tool will display a summary listing the infected items and their descriptions. The tool will automatically select the required action for malicious items (**Cure** or **Delete**), but will let you decide what to do with suspicious objects (**Skip** is selected by default). If you want to quarantine the deleted objects, select **Copy to quarantine**. Note that the files won't be removed.

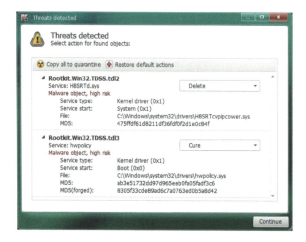

Click on **Continue** to let the tool remove the infections. When the removal is done, TDSSKiller might prompt you to reboot your PC for complete removal of the rootkit. Reboot your computer and everything should be back to normal.

If Kaspersky's tool doesn't remove the Google redirect virus, try Symantec's **FixTDSS.exe**. This tool usually helps when TDSSKiller.exe fails to do the job.

However, sometimes neither of these programs works. That's when you'll need to remove the redirect virus manually.

How to remove the Google redirect virus manually

Like I said, sometimes the software tools fail to remove the Google redirect virus. In that case, you'll need to delete it manually. This process is not the simplest one, but completing these steps works in most cases.

The first thing you will need to do is make your system show hidden files and folders:

Windows XP:

1.   Click on **Start**, then click on **Run...** and type **control folders** in the Run box. Hit Enter
2.   Go to the **View** tab and select **Show hidden files, folders and drives**

3.   Uncheck **Hide extensions for known file types**

4.   Uncheck **Hide protected operating system files**

Windows 7:

1.   Click on **Start** and go to the **Control Panel**

2.Click on **Appearance and Personalization**, then click on **Show hidden files and folders** under **Folder Options**

3.   Select the **Show hidden files, folders, and drives** radio button, then click **Apply**, and then click **OK**

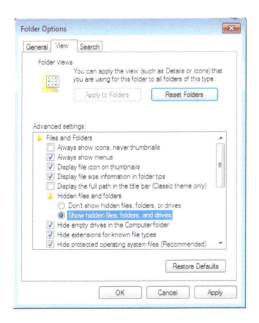

Now we'll need to modify computer startup. To do that, you will need to launch the system configuration utility – **msconfig**:

1.   Click on **Start**, then type **msconfig** in the **Search bar** (XP users click on **Run...** and type **msconfig** there). Press **Enter**

2.		Go to the **Boot** tab (**BOOT.INI** in Windows XP) and check **BOOTLOG**

3.		Reboot your PC to apply the changes and to create the **ntbttxt.log** file, which we will need later on

Now let's open the **Device Manager**:

1.		Click on **Start**, then type **devmgmt.msc** in the **Search bar** (XP users click on **Run…** and type **devmgmt.msc** there). Press **Enter**

2.		Go to the **View** tab and check **Show hidden devices**

3.		Find and expand the **Non-plug and play drivers** to check that the **Show hidden devices** option is enabled for them

4.		Look for an entry called something like **TDSSserv.sys**. If it's there, write down its name

5.		Right-click on the TDSS entry and uninstall it

6.		**DO NOT** restart your computer, even if Windows prompts you to do that

The next thing you'll need to do is open **Registry Editor**:

1.		Click on **Start**, then type **regedit** in the **Search bar** (XP users click on **Run…** and type **regedit** in the box). Press **Enter**

2.		Make a backup of the registry by clicking on **File** and selecting **Export**. Save the backup somewhere on your drive

3.		Now click on **Edit**, select **Find** and type in **TDSS**

4.		If your search returns an entry, delete it. Repeat the search to find and delete other similar entries

5.		If a search returns a file that shows its path, such as C:\Windows\System32\TDSSmain.dll, go to the folder in question and delete the entry from there

6.		If you can't find TDSSmain.dll when you go to System32, you will need to use the command prompt to delete the file

7.		Click on **Start**, **Run…** and type **cmd.exe**. Hit **Enter**. In the command prompt, type **del C:\Windows\System32\TDSSmain.dll** and press **Enter** to delete TDSS

8.   Repeat these steps to find and delete all TDSS entries

Now let's check the log file and make sure there are no infections left. To do that, simply search for the file called **ntbtlog.txt** using Windows search and then review it for any TDSS entries. If you find any of them, open **regedit** and repeat the steps above to completely remove the virus. When finished, reboot your computer.

One thing you need to understand is that the Google redirect virus can be called something other than TDSS. In that case, simply look for weird names with a .sys file extension in the Device Manager. If you find an entry that has a ridiculous name that doesn't make sense (like fksaisdf.sys), you can be pretty sure it's a virus as no legitimate company will call its driver something like that. Simply repeat the steps described above to remove all traces of the virus.

Now you can launch **msconfig** again and uncheck **BOOTLOG**, as you won't need the log anymore. Reboot your computer for the changes to take effect.

Now you know how to remove even the most resilient viruses. So let's move on and discuss the dangers of the World Wide Web.

Dangers of the Web

Phishing, Online Fraud, Scams, Ransomware and Identity Theft

These days 99.9% of computers get infected from the Internet. Some malware comes from infected software or files we download, some gets installed on our computers when we click on links on infected websites, and some malware infects our computers when we install a Facebook app or follow a link on Twitter. That's why you need to use up-to-date security software when you do anything online. But there are other dangers of the Web that even the best security software can't save you from. I'm talking about phishing, online fraud and various scams. So, let's find out what these threats are and how they are executed. And let's find out how you can stay safe.

Phishing

As you've probably guessed, the word "phishing" comes from "fishing". That's because phishing is a technique hackers use to fish out your personal information – your usernames, passwords, and even your credit card details. The way hackers do it is sophisticated and simple at the same time. They simply create websites that look very much like well-known legitimate websites. For example, malicious persons can create a website that is almost identical to your bank's online banking site, a popular online store (such as Amazon.com), a website that looks very much like Facebook... Well, you get the idea. But then why would you visit one of these websites? Of course you wouldn't type a URL of a phishing website in your browser. The answer is that you get tricked into visiting the website.

Most of the time, phishing is carried out by email or instant messaging. A classic phishing case is when you get an email that looks as if it was sent by your bank. This email usually states that you need to take immediate action and change your PIN, update your details, change your password or something of a similar nature. Typically, there is a link for you to click. If you click on this link, you are directed to a phishing website that looks just like your bank's official website and there is a form that you are asked to fill in. Needless to say that as soon as you fill in the form, the fake website's owner has all your bank details. Say goodbye to your money.

One of the most recent popular phishing scams is the US Postal Service scam. Basically, you get an email that has **"Package delivery failure!"** as the subject. In the email, you are told that there is a package for you, but you need to update your address and other details for the package to be delivered. Of course, there is a link for you to click on and that link takes you to a fake US Postal Service website. You are then prompted to enter your details and they get stolen. Not a good scenario.

Luckily, it's pretty easy to avoid phishing because all you need to do is use your common sense. True, a lot of security software programs have anti-phishing features and Internet Explorer scans websites you visit for phishing activity, but what you really need to do is pay attention and double-check everything. Here is what you need to do when you receive a suspicious email:

✓   Never click on any links in suspicious emails. Phishers typically include unsetting information to make you act without thinking. Like, there was a $500 withdrawal from your account from a foreign country. If you get an email that looks like it's from your bank, contact your bank and let them know about it. And if you feel like visiting your bank's website, it's best to type the website's address in your browser's address bar.

✓   If you get an email from a friend's or a colleague's address that doesn't look like it has been written by the person you know and contains a link, let them know immediately. For example, if you get an email with the subject line **"Yo! Check this out!"** from your boss or college tutor, you should know that something is wrong. They are either completely drunk or their email account got hacked and they need to change their password.

✓ Most phishing emails are written in poor English and contain mistakes. If you get an email that is supposed to be from USPS, but has numerous spelling and grammar mistakes, delete it immediately. It's just another phishing scam.

✓ If you suspect that you've landed on a phishing website, don't enter any personal details. First of all check that the website is legitimate. Check for security seals, https:// verification (if the website doesn't have secure and verified https:// connection when it's asking you to enter credit card data, then it's not legitimate), and check the general feel of the website. However, it's best to leave the website and type in the URL you want in the new browser window, as some phishers can forget the https:// and the lock you see at the bottom of your browser.

✓ Install an anti-phishing browser add-on. My favorite is WOT (Web Of Trust). This add-on warns you when you visit websites that have been marked by the community as offensive.

✓ Report phishing to the Internet Crime Complaint Center at http://www.ic3.gov.

Now you know how to avoid phishing. But there is something you need to watch out for that is equally damaging to your wallet – online fraud.

Online fraud and scams

Just like any other type of fraud, the purpose of online fraud is to steal your money. A prospective victim is presented with something that looks very attractive or even legitimate (which it's not). And when the victim is persuaded into purchasing the service or good (or even donate to a non-existent charity), a fraudulent transaction takes place.

Here are some common types of online fraud you need to watch out for:

✓ Purchase fraud – when a buyer commits payment fraud and pays with something like a stolen credit card.

✓   AMMYY scams - this is a phone plus computer scam. Basically, you get a phone call from someone who pretends to be either from a local IT company (despite having a heavy foreign accent) or even Microsoft. The person tells you that your computer has multiple errors and needs fixing. He even prompts you to go to your event log and see these errors for yourself (all event logs have at least a couple of warnings). He then asks your permission to connect to your PC remotely and when he does that he loads your PC with malware, steals your banking details and asks for money for the so-called fix. Since nobody can know if your PC has errors without actually looking at your computer, hang up immediately if you get such a call, or even better - tell them you don't own a computer at all.

✓   Counterfeit postal money orders – when you supposedly receive a large amount of money, but you are asked to pay the commission first. You pay the commission and naturally you never get the money.

✓   Online auction fraud – this includes eBay fraud and PayPal fraud, when the victim pays for a good that never arrives. In other cases, the fraudster collects the good in person while having paid for it via PayPal. Then the fraudster challenges the seller via PayPal and gets a refund from PayPal. PayPal does not protect the seller in such situations and is happy to reverse the payment unless the seller can provide a shipment tracking number.

✓   Money transfer fraud – the victim receives an email from a supposed relative of a deceased relative. The victim is asked to help with money transfer in exchange for a hefty sum of money. The fraudsters send fake checks and money orders and the victim sends the money to scammers before the fraud is discovered.

✓   Work from home scams – typically, the victim is offered a fantastic job opportunity to work from home. Then the scam victim is either asked to pay for training or is required to perform a test task. Naturally, after the payment is received or the job is done, the scammers don't contact the victim ever again.

✓   Dating scams – the recipients of dating scam emails are usually men. They get an email from a woman, typically from an Eastern

European country. When the online relationship develops, the scammers ask for money for an airfare, medicine for the sick mother, and so on.

✓ Florida travel scams – these are the most recent scams in the travel industry that mostly target UK and Australia. The victim gets an email saying that they are entitled to a very cheap holiday in Florida. There is a phone number to call and a link to a website. A phone call confirms that everything seems to be genuine and the victim pays. However, what you are really buying here is a timeshare. On top of that, there is a minimal annual salary requirement of something like $200K/year, which means that most people will never be able to go on that holiday. The money you pay is non-refundable after a 30-day period.

And that's not all – there are many other varieties of online fraud. Luckily, there are some things you can do to protect yourself. Now, all of the above-mentioned ways to protect yourself from phishing work when it comes to protecting yourself from online fraud. Always use your common sense and don't fall for something that looks too good to be true. Remember that you can never buy a Ferrari for the price of a donut.

Ransomware

These days, people don't expect to be demanded to pay a ransom. After all, the time of outlaws attacking merchant caravans is long gone! But if you think that ransom is a thing of the past, you're wrong. The outlaws have now moved to cyberspace and created ransomware.

Ransomware is a type of malware that sneaks into your operating system and blocks access to your files or even your entire computer until the ransom is paid. Needless to say, payment doesn't always guarantee that the files get unblocked.

Just like other malware attacks, a typical ransomware attack starts with the user downloading the infection from the Internet. That can happen when a user visits an infected website, downloads an attachment from an infected email, clicks on a fake ad and so on. Often ransomware is downloaded as part of a malware 'package'. That's why you have to be extremely careful and never click on suspicious links.

Once ransomware is executed on a system, it either completely locks the computer or locks certain file types. When the user tries to access the computer or the locked files, a pop-up appears and tells the user that he or she must pay to get the files decrypted. Usually, payment is processed through cryptocurrency like bitcoin, which lets the attackers stay anonymous.

You can protect your computer from getting infected by ransomware just like you protect it from any other malware. This includes installing an antimalware solution, keeping it updated and, most importantly, being careful when you use the Internet.

Online identity theft

Identity theft is becoming a major concern as more and more people have their identity stolen. That's because it's become really easy to get hold of your personal data online and the chances of the criminal getting caught are next to none.

While there is no universal recipe for preventing online identity theft, there are several things you can do to minimize the risk of your personal data being stolen. Here are a few tips that will help you stay protected.

The first thing you should remember is that you need good security software. When it comes to protecting yourself from identity theft, not all anti-virus programs are the same. Some of them only have basic features and don't offer protection against spyware, phishing, and keyloggers (programs that record everything you type, including your passwords). That's why you should make sure your security software includes privacy protection and has a strong behavioral scanner. Remember that a good all-round security suite should have anti-spyware, anti-phishing, and anti-keylogging tools alongside real-time protection and privacy control features.

Another thing that can help you avoid online identity theft is strong passwords. I've already covered how to create a strong password in chapter two.

In this chapter, I'm going to give you some extra tips for protecting your accounts. The first thing you should remember is to never use the same password for different online accounts. This will help you stay safe even if one of your passwords falls into the hands of malicious persons. This is especially true for your online banking account. And if you have trouble remembering all the complex passwords you've created, use software like KeyPass, LastPass or RoboForm to manage them.

And last but not least, never share your bank details with anyone online. Whether you are using the Internet to buy or sell good, you should never share your bank details with anyone.

There are plenty of secure online payment methods, from using prepaid VISA and MasterCard cards to using online payment systems, such as PayPal, and Skrill to name a couple. These payment systems only require an email address to send or receive payments, which makes them secure and easy to use.

Now you know how to protect yourself from phishing, online fraud and scams, and online identity theft. But did you know that you could get infected through your browser?

How You Can Get Infected Through Your Browser

Protect Yourself from Browser Infections

Wouldn't it be great if there was no way your computer could get infected via your Web browser! Just imagine how much easier life would be if browsers ran webpages in a way that totally separated them from the rest of your computer, so that no infection could creep in. Unfortunately, we don't live in the perfect world. Malicious websites exploit browser and plugin vulnerabilities to install bad stuff on your computer. Worse still, they often use social engineering tactics to trick the users and make them install the malware with their own mouse clicks. Let's have a look at how malware installs itself on your PC and what you can do to prevent it from happening.

Browser plugins

The most common way for malware to get installed through your browser is exploiting insecure browser plugins.

Plugins are juicy targets because their vulnerabilities can be exploited in lots of ways, in any browser, on any operating system. For example, a Flash plugin vulnerability could be used to compromise Google Chrome, Mozilla Firefox, or Internet Explorer running on Windows, Linux, or Mac.

Java is by far the worst and the most dangerous. Just for you to get the idea, recently Apple and Facebook had their internal computers compromised because employees accessed websites that contained malicious Java applets. And don't start giggling and thinking "They should have updated their Java". Their Java plugins could have been completely up-to-date because the latest Java version still contains unpatched security holes.

So, if you want to protect yourself, you should completely uninstall Java from your computer. It's easily done from the Control Panel. If you need it for something you use, then at least disable the Java browser plugin. Here is how:

1.   Press the **Windows key**, type **Java** and press **Enter** to open the **Java Control Panel**. Windows 8 users will need to go to the **Settings** category after typing **Java**.
2.   Go to the **Security** tab and uncheck the **Enable Java content in the browser** checkbox.
3.   This will disable the Java plug-in in all your installed browsers, although downloaded applications will still be able to use Java.

4.   Click **OK** to apply the changes

But Java is not the only super dangerous browser plugin. Other extensions, especially Adobe's Flash player and PDF reader browser plugins, are also prone to vulnerabilities and have to be patched on a regular basis. Adobe has become better than Oracle at issuing timely fixes and patches, but Flash vulnerability exploits are still very common.

To protect yourself from plugin vulnerabilities, make sure you:

• Use a website like Firefox plugin check to see if any of your plugins are outdated. This website works on Firefox and other browsers, even though it was developed by Mozilla.

• If you find any outdated plugins, update them immediately. Enable automatic updates to ensure that you always have the latest versions.
• Uninstall unused plugins. Doing that will help you reduce the "attack surface" because it will lower the amount of software that can be exploited on your computer.
• Use the click-to-play plugins feature in Chrome or Firefox. Using this feature will prevent plugins from running when you don't specifically request them to.
• Use an anti-virus and configure it to download automatic updates. This will not only protect you from zero-day threats, but will also help you get rid of an infection if your computer gets one.

Browser security vulnerabilities

Even though browsers have largely fixed security problems and these days it's mostly the plugins that are dangerous, browser vulnerabilities can still compromise your computer.

However, this doesn't mean that you should sit back and relax. If you are using an old and unpatched version of Internet Explorer 6 or an outdated version of Safari, any malicious website you visit could exploit security holes in your browser to install malware without your permission or knowledge.

Keeping an eye on browser security vulnerabilities is not at all hard. The first thing that you should remember is to keep your browser updated. These days most browsers download and install updated automatically, so make sure you leave the autoupdate feature enabled. And since Internet Explorer is updated using Windows Update, make sure you have it set to Automatic too.

Another thing you should do is have an updated anti-virus. Just like with the plugins, an anti-virus will keep your computer protected from zero-day threats.

Social engineering

A lot of cyber criminals use social engineering tactics. That is, they convince you to install malware on your computer by offering you a fake update, prompting you to click on fake download links and even opening dangerous email attachments.

The ways how people are tricked vary, but here are the most popular social engineering techniques cyber criminals use:

• **A bogus ActiveX control** - Internet Explorer uses ActiveX controls. That's OK. But what's not OK is that any website can ask you to download an ActiveX control. Most of the time they are legitimate and are needed for something, like watching a Flash video online. But it's also how people are tricked into downloading malware.

• **Auto-download files** - a lot of malicious files will attempt to automatically make your computer download an executable file in hope that you will be tempted to run it. When that happens to you, leave the website immediately and delete the file right away.

• **Fake plugins** - another favored tactic is displaying a message that you need to download a plugin or a video codec to watch a really cool video. While this can be perfectly legitimate, be careful and don't download anything from untrusted websites before checking it first.

• **Fake download links** - usually bogus download links appear on low quality, untrusted websites. But sometimes they creep in on perfectly safe websites as ads. So be careful. Software download websites and sites containing pirated content are usually the target.

• **Fake warning messages** - these include the famous "Your computer is infected!", "Your computer has critical errors!" and "Your computer has been locked!" messages. Don't trust them, leave the sites that display them and scan your computer with an anti-virus for good measure.

This list is not extensive, but it gives you an idea what to stay away from. And remember that having a good anti-virus can save everything even if you do download and try to install a malicious program by mistake. The anti-virus will detect malicious activity and quarantine the malware.

Now let's move on and see what you can do to protect yourself from any nasty surprises when doing your shopping online.

Don't Break Your Leg on an Online Shopping Spree

How to Stay Safe When Shopping Online

Do you do all your shopping locally? I bet that's not quite true and you do a fair bit of your shopping online. When it comes to buying gadgets, DVDs, books, home appliances and zillions of other things, nothing can beat online stores. They usually have a wider range of goods and their prices easily beat every discount your local stores can afford to offer. Not to mention the convenience of having everything delivered to your doorstep. That's why more and more people do their shopping online. In fact, a lot of stores and supermarkets had to open Web stores to meet with the demands of the market. As a result, a lot of people shop for everything, from food to clothes and furniture, online.

To cut a long story short, online shopping is a great and convenient way to buy things. However, there is one thing that makes online shopping not as attractive as actual shopping and that thing is safety. You see, there are a lot of bogus online stores and there are a lot of people who want nothing but steal your money. On top of that, there are a lot of stores that sell low-quality goods while making them sound great.

When you receive such goods, the store doesn't want to hear about refunds or returns and claims that it was mentioned in their policy (very few people read Terms of Service and Policies for websites they visit). And, naturally, there is always the fact that online shopping is always a bit of a gamble, since you can't hold, test, or try on the goods you are buying. Nevertheless, there are ways of protecting yourself from disappointments when shopping online. More importantly, there are ways to stay safe and avoid online fraud and shopping scams.

The first thing you should remember is to always shop from trusted, well-known online stores. There are a lot of dubious sites that offer amazing bargains. In fact, some of them are too amazing to be genuine. There are a lot of websites that only pretend to be shops, but all they want is to steal your money.

Remember, nobody is going to offer you a laptop for the price of a cup of coffee. Therefore, it's strongly recommended to shop only from sites you know. Also it doesn't hurt to double-check any shops that you found with the help of Google. Never enter your payment details unless you are absolutely sure the site is legitimate.

Always pay attention to security seals, shipping, return, and refund policies, and check whether the site uses secure connection (https://) when you are asked to enter payment details. And don't forget to look up unfamiliar shops on Google and read user reviews. If the shop is fraudulent, then there will be lots of users complaining online.

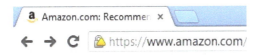

Never buy anything advertised via unsolicited email and never click on any links in such emails either. These emails are almost always a scam and links take you to websites that infect your computer with viruses. If a website asks you to wire money or send a money order, close it and forget all about it if you don't want to be ripped off.

Control spam

A lot of people who like doing their shopping online often complain about retailers keeping sending them news and offers even if they never subscribe to any.

This usually happens if you don't pay attention to which checkboxes you select and what sort of terms you agree to. However, some unscrupulous online retailers do spam their customers and even share your details with third party companies.

If you are concerned about being spammed by online retailers, you can always either create a separate email address for online shopping, or create aliases. Here's how it's done in Gmail.

Let's say your address is myemail@gmail.com and you are shopping at a website called bestdeal.com. So, when they ask for your email address, type it as myemail+bestdeal@gmail.com. This way all future emails from this shop will be addressed to myemail+bestdeal@gmail.com. If the shop starts sending you spam or emails from third party stores start coming to that address, you will know who shared your details and will be able to take action.

Protect your payment details

When shopping online, there is always a concern that your financial information may be stolen and unauthorized payments may start occurring. That's why you should always take extra care and protect your payment details.

The easiest way to protect yourself is to pay with a credit card. Most people have several bank cards, including credit and debit. Both can be used for online shopping, but it's safer to use a credit card.

That's because credit card companies make it easier to deal with the bank if there are any unauthorized charges. In most cases the bank will give you your money back without even issuing a fine, whereas there may be a lot of fines and overdraft interest charges if you use a debit card.

But there is an even safer payment option – prepaid cards. These are cards issued by the major payment systems, such as VISA and MasterCard, that are not tied to any particular account. You simply load them with money whenever you want and then you can safely hop online and start spending. Even if there is a fraudulent transaction, it's only your prepaid card balance that may suffer. Since the card is not connected with any of your other accounts, they will stay safe. And the best bit is that there are no overdraft charges, as the system stops processing payments when your balance reaches zero.

Another great payment option is using a virtual VISA card. A card like that works just like a physical prepaid card. The only difference is that the virtual card only exists on your computer screen. The fact that the card is virtual makes it cheaper to maintain, cuts down the fees you have to pay and makes using it more secure because all your financial information is encrypted. On top of that, it's really easy to cancel a virtual card and get a new one with a new number in seconds. There are several companies that provide prepaid virtual VISA cards, EntroPay being the most popular and trusted one. It's a UK-based company regulated by the FSA (Financial Services Authority) that works in association with VISA.

But then again, you don't even have to share your credit, debit or a prepaid card details when you do your shopping online – there are plenty of alternative payment methods that allow you to protect your privacy when shopping online. You can use online payment systems, such as PayPal, Google Checkout, Amazon Payments, Payza, Skrill and lots more. There are also options to pay using gift cards and certificates, pay in cash upon delivery if you choose courier delivery method, or even use websites like billmelater.com (a PayPal service) that allow you to shop online without having to enter your bank card details. A lot of online retailers encourage you to use such services by offering free shipping and an option to postpone your payment for up to 6 months.

Now you should be safe when shopping online. But what about the safety of your email and online accounts? In the next chapter, I'm going to give you some tips on how you can protect your online accounts and fight spam.

Keep Your Keys to Yourself

Protect Your Email and Online Accounts

These days using email is even more common than using a landline phone – not everybody has a landline, but pretty much everybody uses email. Same goes for other online accounts, such as Facebook, Twitter, LinkedIn and Google+. Email and social networks are a great way to communicate with your family and friends, keep in touch with classmates, colleagues, and find new friends. On top of that, social networks are great for finding out the most recent news and sharing information.

But there is one big problem. You see, as more people start using social networks, more and more malicious persons use social networks too. They load social network websites with apps infected with malware, create elaborate scams and spam other users. As for email, then every single email user has encountered spam more than once. Luckily, there are several things you can do to protect yourself from spam and keep your online accounts secure.

Protecting your email accounts

Most likely you have more than one email accounts – one personal and one for work. And if you use just one email account for both individual and business use, then you should stop that and create a separate account for your business. This will help you be more organized and will help you avoid getting tons of spam sent to your business email address. But how do you get spam in the first place?

We all get spam and we all hate it. There is nothing worse than logging into your email account and finding something like 60 spam messages there. They can be everything, but most of the time spam messages are of an insulting nature, promoting things like Viagra and sex services. Don't know about you, but it's definitely not what I want to see in my email Inbox or even in the Spam folder.

Luckily, there are several things you can do to cut the amount of spam right down and block some of the most annoying messages. The first thing you should do is start being careful and avoid leaving your email address for everyone to see. Whatever you do, don't post your email address anywhere but secure forms because hackers scour the Web for email addresses. Posting your email address for the world to see is a sure way to start receiving tons of spam and the worst imaginable phishing scam emails. And if you have no choice and have to post your email address, change "@" to "at" and "." to "dot" and put some spaces in. This will make the email address unreadable to bots.

Get an extra email account

One of the ways of dealing with spam is creating a separate email account for newsletter subscriptions, registering on various websites, entering online competitions, and even online shopping. Having a separate email address for these things can save you a lot of time and let you avoid frustration. I know how annoying it is to waste time identifying spam messages among your personal or even business emails. Not only does it get on your nerves, but you also risk deleting an important message by mistake. I know that because it happened to me on numerous occasions. That's why I strongly advise you to create an extra email account for website registrations and so on.

You can use any of the free email providers you like. Personally, I prefer using Gmail because Yahoo and Hotmail addresses often block email verification messages sent by some websites. They also are not accepted by some online stores. And Gmail is the most secure free email, which is always a bonus.

Now you won't have to worry about sorting through your emails because it won't matter whether that account gets spammed or not. Just log in to that account occasionally and delete messages in bulk.

Block spam

Even though creating a special email account for registrations and newsletter subscriptions can greatly minimize the amount of spam you get to your other email accounts, it's hard to stop spam altogether. In fact, it's a constant battle that you need to keep fighting. Nevertheless, there are things you can do to block spam's way.

All Web email accounts have the option to blacklist and block email addresses. This means that you can configure your email account to block all messages coming from spamming email addresses, so that they never reach you. Here is how it's done on Gmail, Yahoo and Hotmail.

Gmail:

1.   Log into your Gmail account and go to **Mail Settings** by clicking on the **Settings** icon in the upper right corner

2.   Click on the **Filters** link and then click on **Create a new filter**

3.   If you know the email address where the spam keeps coming from, simply enter it in the **From** field. If not, but you know that you don't want any Viagra spam, simply enter the word "Viagra" in the **Includes the words** field

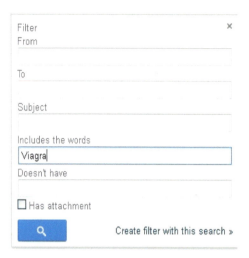

4.   Click on the **Create filter with this search** link

5.   You will be asked to select the action that will always be performed when an email containing the word "Viagra" comes your way

6.   Check the **Delete it** checkbox

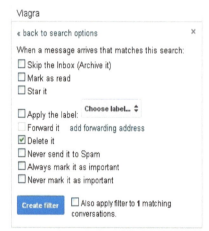

7.   Click on the **Create Filter** button and Viagra spam won't ever bother you again

You can edit the filter at any time by going to **Filters**.

Yahoo

1.   Log into your Yahoo email account, click on **Options** and then on **Mail Options**

2.   If you know the spammer's email address, then click on **Blocked Addresses** in the menu on the left

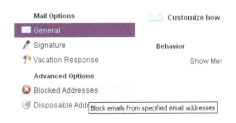

3.   Enter the offender's email address and click on the **+** sign. The address will be added to the list of your blocked addresses

You can also create a filter to filter out emails with offending content:

1.   Log into your Yahoo email account, click on **Options** and then on **Mail Options**

2.   Click on the **Filters** item in the menu on the left

3.   Click on the **Add** button to add a filter

4.   Now name the filter and enter that **Email body Contains Viagra** under **If all of the following rules are true**. Leave the rest of the fields blank

5.   Then select **Trash** from the drop-down menu under **Then deliver the email to the following folder**

6.   Your settings will be saved automatically when you navigate away from the page

Outlook.com (Hotmail)

1.   Log into your Outlook.com (Hotmail) account, click on the **Options** icon, then on **More email settings**

2.   Under **Preventing junk emails** click on **Safe and blocked senders**

3.   Click on **Blocked senders**

4.   In the **Blocked email address or domain** field type in the address you want to block

5.   Click on **Add to list** and the email address will be added to the list of your blocked senders

Now you know how to deal with spam, which means that it's time to learn how to protect your online accounts from being hacked.

Protecting your online accounts from being hacked

Having your accounts hacked is probably one of the worst things that can happen to you online. If you are lucky, the hacker will only mess up your profiles on sites like Facebook and LinkedIn, which may damage your online reputation. But if your online banking accounts get hacked, the consequences can be a lot more serious. That's why it's so important to protect your online accounts and avoid being hacked in the first place. Here are a few tips that will help you.

I've already talked a lot about the importance of using strong passwords, but I just have to mention it once again. Using strong passwords can save you a lot of trouble and make sure practical jokers won't be able to access your email accounts, social media profiles, and your online banking page. To create strong passwords, remember to use alpha-numerical combinations that mean something to you, but can't be guessed by anyone else. Also remember to use different passwords for different accounts and change all your passwords at least every two months.

Unfortunately, even the strongest passwords will not protect you from serious hackers, as they have means to crack literally any password. That is, unless you keep your passwords encrypted using software like SensiGuard, KeyPass, TrueCrypt or use a password manager like LastPass or RoboForm.

Another way to protect your online accounts is to use two-factor authentication. Using two-factor authentication will keep your accounts safe even if someone lays their hands on your passwords. That's because two-factor authentication means that you need more than just your password to access your account - you will also need to enter a special code that is usually sent to you by SMS or generated by a mobile app.

A number of different services support two-factor authentication, including Facebook, Google and Dropbox. Also most online banking systems require two-factor authentication. While using it means you need more time to access your account, it's highly recommended. And usually you will only need it if you are logging in from an unrecognized computer, as most online services allow you to remember your access token.

In addition to using two-factor authentication, I recommend configuring your Gmail, Facebook and Twitter accounts to send you an email or an SMS every time someone logs into your account from an unauthorized device. Configuring these notifications only takes a minute and their benefits are obvious. If someone hacks your account you will have enough time to log in and change your password before the intruder locks you out of your own account and steals your information.

You can configure login notifications under **Security Settings** on Facebook, **Accounts and Import** on Gmail and **Settings - Mobile** on Twitter.

Another thing you should do is be careful of what you download and which sites you download from. Everybody loves downloading free stuff from the Internet, be it software, music, or eBooks. I know I do – I'm constantly on the lookout for freebies and interesting reads! While a lot of free downloads are legitimate and are perfectly safe, quite a few are infested by spyware and keyloggers that are there to steal your personal information. That's why you should never download anything from unknown and untrusted websites. Legitimate downloads are usually available from websites like Download.com and have a badge that they are free of spyware, adware, and any other malicious code.

Protect your Facebook account

Facebook is the most popular social networking site out there and I'm sure you're on it. Because Facebook is so popular and because most people love sharing personal information on it, it's an all-time favorite site for initiating hacker attacks. Thousands of people had their Facebook accounts hacked and even Mark Zuckerberg's account got hacked once.

To be honest, Facebook is doing a pretty good job trying to update its privacy settings and stop the attacks. For example, now every user is required to provide a working phone number. However, there is still room for improvement and you can do a lot to protect your account by configuring some settings.

The first thing you should do is configure Facebook to always use SSL encryption. By default, the website uses HTTPS only when you enter your password. But now it's possible to ask Facebook to use a secure connection when possible. This option is especially useful if you use public Wi-Fi connections to access your account.

To enable HTTPS on Facebook, go to **Account Settings** and select **Security** on the left-hand side. You will see whether **Secure Browsing** is on or off. If it's disabled, click **Edit** and check the checkbox to enable it. Click on **Save Changes** and you're done.

Now that you have HTTPS enabled, your Facebook account should be more secure. But only too often users endanger themselves by not paying attention to which apps and games they give permissions to. In the past, a lot of the applications and games on Facebook contained malicious code and were designed to steal your information and hijack your account. Now the situation is somewhat better because Facebook started using randomly generated app passwords to ensure security. App passwords are one-time passwords you use to log into your apps without having to enter your Facebook password.

To get an app password, go to your **Account Settings**, and then click on **Security**. Click **Edit** next to **App Passwords** and follow the prompts. This will help you keep your account more secure.

Another thing you should do is carefully read which permissions an app requires before you agree to grant them. I know that reading all that stuff is pretty boring, but it may really pay off. Pay extra attention to apps that request the ability to write on your wall, post status updates or even message your friends. Ask yourself why an app would want these permissions and think of the behavior you are expecting from it. If it seems suspicious, don't risk it and don't agree to use the app.

But even if you have a strong password, use HTTPS and don't use any malicious apps, you could be putting yourself at risk by posting too much information. For example, posting your birth date seems harmless, but it can be used by hackers as a way to get into your other accounts, as birth date is often used as a security question. And your location may be used to not only things like physical attacks, but to con you into sharing more information.

Imagine that a hacker sends you a message saying something like "Hi, we met at a conference in [name of place] last week. Could you provide more information about your company?", etc.
You will be surprised by the number of people who disclosed a lot of personal information this way.

And last but not least, don't forget to log out of your Facebook account. I know that staying logged in is convenient, but logging out can save you from becoming a victim of a **likejacking** attack - a worm that uses your account to like pages.

How to detect a hacker attack

No security software is perfect and even the best anti-virus or Internet security suite can miss infections. Same goes for your firewall when it comes to hacker attacks. I think there is no need for me to tell you how dangerous hacker attacks are, especially if your business computer gets attacked.

The worst bit about hacker attacks is that a hacker can be accessing every single bit of information on your computer with you none the wiser. Luckily, there are ways of detecting a hacker attack – you just need to keep an eye on what's going on and monitor your computer for any suspicious activity. Anyway, here are some things to watch out for.

Suspiciously high outgoing traffic for dial-up, mobile broadband and ADSL is the first thing that should attract your attention, especially if you're not uploading anything at the time. So, if you notice that your outgoing traffic is all of a sudden unusually high, it could mean that your computer has been compromised and used either to send spam or viruses to all your contacts, or simply sends your private information to the hacker. Cable users, don't fret – with cable it is quite normal to have the same amount of outgoing and incoming traffic.

Even if your outgoing traffic seems OK, you should regularly look out for strange-looking files in the root directories of your drives. In addition to that, monitor your computer for excessive disk activity. Usually hackers run a thorough scan of your system after they've successfully hacked into it. They do it to find and access your personal information like passwords, credit card details, PayPal account details etc. So, increased disk activity and suspicious files can be an indication that your system has either been hacked or is infected with malware.

Sometimes you might get constant alerts form your firewall reporting blocking large packets of data from the same IP address. That almost always means that someone is probing your defenses and is trying to break in. There is one good thing about it, though - if your firewall is blocking the attacks, then it most likely will continue to do so. Just keep it up-to-date.

And last but not least, keep your security software updated and run regular scans. A lot of hackers still rely on Trojans and backdoors, so make sure your system is free of them.

Having strong passwords, good security software and being cautious is a lot. But it's not really enough if you use cloud computing at home or at work.

How to Protect Your Data

Protect Your Files Both Online and Offline

Cloud computing is already part of our lives, both at home and at work. Everybody uses the Cloud for at least some tasks, and some enterprises migrated a lot of their data to the Cloud to optimize workflow. However, cloud computing is not as secure as we like to think and can lead to a lot of problems when used without proper consideration and security measures.

Five security sins of cloud computing

There are a lot of common cloud computing security mistakes that both home and business users make. Are you making them?

Failing to check IDs in a proper way

 In an enterprise, the only really secure way to log into the Cloud is by using the company's identity management systems. And if your company has one, then you should definitely be using it. Even though a lot of cloud services have an option to allow pretty much any employee to sign up, create their own login credentials without registering them with the enterprise, and then connect these credentials to personal email addresses, that doesn't mean that it's the right way to do it and should be allowed. Doing this is asking for trouble, as it creates the perfect conditions for information leaks and security vulnerabilities.

Similarly, some businesses that are deploying IaaS do so in a pretty irresponsible manner. They use self-service capabilities, which is an easy way to allow unguarded access to cloud service. Again, that's something that should never be done. What if it's a customer-facing cloud service? Then any customer or any hacker will be able to gain access to the server.

Even if you are a home user, you shouldn't allow anyone to be able to register with your Cloud service and have admin credentials (not that many people would allow that). So, in a way, enterprises are sometimes less secure than an average home computer.

Unprotected API keys

When a business decides to move to the cloud, some users will require APIs (application programming interfaces) to uniquely use the company's services to their best advantage. The Cloud makes it really easy for the customer to access and use internal services and capabilities, and API integration is great for that.

The use of APIs is very common now. For example, if you are a WordPress blogger and use some automatic Twitter plugins, you should be familiar with Twitter API. Same goes for mobile developers.

The important things you need to understand about APIs is that they are used to access different services, which means that they can be compared to passwords. You know what happens if you lose your passwords, right? So keep in mind that cloud service APIs need to be protected really well.

Forgetting to be independent of cloud providers

As various cloud services evolve and new companies emerge, the cloud patriarchs like Facebook and Amazon are adopting their best practices as standards and make them available on a smaller scale. But that's not the reason for your company to adopt these practices straight away because cloud computing is constantly evolving and the best way today may not be the best choice in the future. Sometimes it even makes sense to move applications back from the Cloud. So, if you feel that the cloud services you are using are not secure enough or not offering all the functionality that you need, consider other choices that will work better for you.

Thinking that the cloud takes away all risks

The Cloud allows companies to move some infrastructure online for faster and easier access. But it's important to understand that outsourcing functionality doesn't mean that you are outsourcing the risks and accountability. So you should always work out risk models with your Cloud provider before you move some features to the Cloud. When you start doing this, you will see that not all Cloud providers are suitable for your particular needs. Remember that a lot of Cloud providers will not take any responsibilities for anything.

Overestimating cloud security

All cloud services tell us how they can make our lives easier, store our data online for convenient access from any computer, make sharing files really easy and so on. But almost none tell the consumer what they are doing to keep our data safe. OK, so we protect our cloud accounts with a password. But you already know that passwords are easy to break. So, if your cloud service provider doesn't offer any additional security, your files can be easily compromised.

Quite often cloud service providers attend to the basic levels of security. They usually depend on automated security applications and platforms. Other companies prefer to outsource higher levels of security to third party providers, which means that it will be very hard for you to dispute the case if someone hacks your data.

That's why you need to make sure that your data is well protected and stored safely. Look for a cloud service provider that is clear about their security policies and offers data encryption.

But even if you don't use the Cloud to store important files, they can easily be compromised and accessed by anyone. Why? Because your data likes to hide in the most unlikely places. These places are something nobody ever thinks of and nobody ever checks. Except for data thieves and cybercriminals, that is.

Three places your data likes to hide

There are many ways for hackers to access your data. From autosaved spreadsheets to SharePoint and test systems, your data can leak out and cause real damage. Real world exposure occurs on a daily basis and there are a lot of vulnerabilities that can easily be exploited. We all know about complicated malware attacks on companies, but nobody ever really tells us how careless employees and plain consumer technology create very real security risks.

Let's have a look at the most unexpected places data likes to hide and avoid the protective eye of security systems.

Spreadsheets

Spreadsheets often contain very sensitive data - financial information, credit card numbers, billing information and so on. You know this.

But did you know that if you don't protect your spreadsheets with a password all this confidential data could be accessed by hackers? Probably not.

When you share spreadsheets via email, file sharing and collaboration services and so on, the data could end up anywhere unless it's properly encrypted. People constantly ask for trouble by failing to encrypt their spreadsheets and saving them on USB thumb drives, DVDs, printing them out and leaving them lying around, and so on. Even if the only place where your spreadsheets are is your hard drive, you should still remember that laptops can be stolen and unless the disk is encrypted, your files could end up in the wrong hands.

But even if you are pretty careful with your spreadsheets, there is something that can still compromise their security - autosave settings. In Microsoft Excel, autosave is enabled by default, which means that the program creates a shadow copy of your spreadsheet on your system as a backup. Basically, it creates a file that can be accessed by anyone.

I wouldn't recommend turning off autosave, but you should remember that it's there and run Windows history cleanup on a regular basis to delete unneeded autosave files.

SharePoint

SharePoint is Microsoft's file sharing, collaboration, and content-and-project-management tool.
It's very versatile and can handle more than 200 file types without you having to customize anything. That's a good thing. But the bad thing is that it can also let tons of confidential data wander free.

Companies use SharePoint to enable data sharing outside the enterprise. Some companies forget to create proper access controls and implement other essential security settings, which makes all that confidential data literally unguarded.

And that's how critical information ends up all over the place. This is not only very dangerous, but it can also cause a lot of embarrassment even if nothing actually gets stolen. For example, I knew some companies that allowed customers to view all transactional data by mistake.

Dropbox and the likes

Dropbox is a very popular service. And even those who don't use Dropbox are likely to use a similar service - OneDrive, Google Drive, SkyDrive, Box, etc. All these services are very easy to use and are free. That certainly does appeal to the customer. But they are not really safe.

When a service like Dropbox starts sending information to the Internet and mobile devices, your confidential information can potentially be accessed by those who don't have proper authorization. This is especially dangerous if you are using Dropbox for business because your confidential data could end up on a public Web server.

Plus Dropbox-like services have another weakness - passwords. Hackers can easily guess weak passwords or get hold of your username and passwords through email scams and other social engineering techniques.

But there is one thing that makes it super-easy for them to hack your account - you reusing your other passwords on Dropbox. Never do that and make sure your Dropbox account has a strong and unique password. And if you store important files in your cloud account, make sure you encrypt them first and upload them next. This way even if a hacker accesses your account, he will still have a hard time opening important files. In fact, you'd be better off not storing any confidential data online at all - better safe than sorry.

But there is something you can do to ensure the ultimate protection of your most sensitive files – encrypt them. So, let's learn about encryption and how it works.

Outsmarting Hackers

How to Use Encryption to Protect Your Files

Did you like adventure and detective stories when you were a kid? If you did, you must have used some sort of secret language and coded letters to share "top secret information" with your friends. Anyway, let's get more to the point and talk about computers. But you know what, using a code to protect your computer is a very good idea. I'm talking about using encryption to protect your private information from prying eyes.

First of all let me explain how computer encryption works. Did you know that you are using encryption without even noticing it? That's because using the Internet also means using encryption. When you are online, you don't just click around and view pages – you check your emails, do your banking online, purchase things at online stores, etc. Well, every time you are entering private information, such as your password or your credit card details, you are using encryption. That is, the website that requires you to enter sensitive information uses encryption to protect you. The Internet has become a dangerous place and websites need to do their bit to protect your privacy. Otherwise nobody would be using online stores and other websites that require authentication.

Anyway, let me remind you what encryption is. Encryption is a method of transforming information using an algorithm to make it unreadable by anyone who doesn't have the key. The encrypted information can only be read with the help of the key or it needs to be fully decrypted. Typically, you would use the same software to encrypt and decrypt your information.

For many years encryption was only used by organizations like governments, the military and secret services. But the rapid development of the Internet required organizations like email providers, social networks, online stores and other websites that need to maintain a high level of security to use encryption as well. Put simply, most businesses use encryption these days because the security risks are very high.

For example, the Computer Security Institute reported that in 2007, 71% of the surveyed companies used encryption for some of their transmitted data, while 53% of surveyed businesses utilized encryption for some of their data in storage. And the number of businesses using encryption is rising. Data theft happens too often these days and too many times customers' personal records have been exposed because of loss and theft of laptops, as well as through information stored on insecure backup drives. That's why businesses don't feel comfortable not using encryption anymore.

Types of encryption

Generally speaking, there are two types of encryption:

• Symmetric encryption – this type of encryption uses the same key to encrypt and decrypt data. It's not as secure as more advanced encryption types, but it's very easy to understand and use. Examples of this encryption method are simple ciphers and 56-bit encryption (DES).

AES (Advanced Encryption Standard) is another symmetric encryption algorithm. This algorithm is approved by the U.S. government and is used worldwide thanks to the high security level it offers combined with ease of use. AES uses key sizes of 128, 192 or 256 bits, 256-bit encryption being the most advanced of them all. When AES encryption was being developed, speed and performance were among the requirements. That's why 256-bit AES encryption works quickly on all types of systems.

• Asymmetric encryption – this encryption method is more advanced because it uses different keys to encrypt and decrypt. Typically, one key is published and is public, whereas the other remains secret. Think of the public key as a padlock and of the private key as the key. When a message is sent, it's like locking a padlock, which only the recipient will be able to unlock. The private key is always kept with the recipient, which makes this encryption method a lot more secure than symmetric encryption. Examples of this encryption method are RSA, a patented U.S.-government supported system, and PGP.

As for what is being encrypted, there are two main encryption methods – full disk encryption and file encryption.

Full disk encryption encrypts every single bit of data stored on a drive. To access the data, a password or a USB token with the decryption key is required at boot up. Needless to say that full disk encryption is an excellent way to prevent unauthorized access. If the computer is stolen or lost, all the data, including the operating system, can't be accessed without the decryption key or password. That's why full disk encryption is a lot more secure than file and folder encryption, which protects only a handful of information and leaves the whole system vulnerable to theft, hackers and malicious software attacks. This is the reason why full disk encryption is essential when a robust security solution is required.

The key benefits of full disk encryption are pre-boot authentication support, minimal risk of data theft, and total security even when the cryptography keys are deleted, as losing the key makes all data unreadable.

In addition to that, some full disk encryption programs include a Trusted Platform Module (TPM), which matches the hard drive with a particular motherboard. This technology is the most effective way of ensuring data is not accessible if the hard drive is stolen and inserted into a different computer.

Full disk encryption is very advanced, but it's also costly. That's why it's mostly used by businesses, whereas file and folder encryption is used by both businesses and individuals.

How to encrypt your files

Encrypting your files and folders is very easy provided you have the right software tools. There are a lot of encryption solutions on the market, so you can choose the software you like best. As a rule, look for an easy to use encryption application that has an intuitive interface and uses 256-bit AES encryption. I recommend using SensiGuard if you are on a Windows-based PC and using TrueCrypt if you are on a Mac.

Encrypting files on a Windows PC

SensiGuard is a program that can be used even by novice users. It has a very clear interface, works quickly and uses 256-bit AES encryption. With this program, you can protect your files, folders, USB devices and even your entire drive. Here is how you can encrypt files with SensiGuard:

1.   Launch SensiGuard by double-clicking on the SensiGuard shortcut on your desktop.

You will be prompted to enter your password. Type in your password and click **OK**. The SensiGuard application window will be displayed

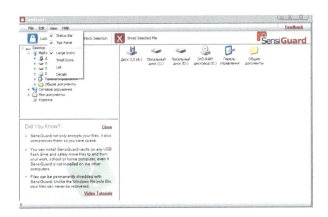

2.   Browse to the files or folders you wish to lock either using the tree structure in the left-hand pane or using the icons in the right-hand pane

3.   Select the file or folder you wish to lock

4.   To lock the file or folder, click on the **Lock** button that is located at the top of the program window

5.   Alternatively, select the file to be locked, click on **Edit** in the menu and select **Lock** from the drop-down list that appears

You can also encrypt files using SensiGuard without having to launch the program – all you need to do is use SensiGuard Windows Explorer context menu options:

1.   Browse to the file or folder you want to lock and right-click on it
2.   Select SensiGuard from the context menu and select **Lock** from the pop-out submenu that appears
3.   The selected file/folder will be locked

To unlock files, simply revert the process.

In addition to encryption options, SensiGuard has a built-in file shredder, which is very handy for deleting files containing confidential information.

Encrypting files on a Mac

Every Mac computer comes with built-in disk encryption software, FileVault. It uses XTS-AES 128 block cipher technology to protect your data. When FileVault protection is enabled, everything on your startup disk is encrypted. You are also required to enter your password every time you start your Mac and your data can't be accessed without your password. Encryption is linked to your password and recovery key.

To check if FileVault is enabled on your Mac, do the following:

1.　　Click on the **Apple icon** and go to **System Preferences**

2.　　Now click on **Security & Privacy**

3.　　　Go to the **FileVault tab** and see if FileVault is enabled

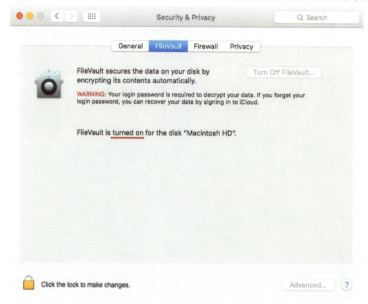

If FileVault disabled and you want to enable it, follow these instructions:

1.　　　Complete the steps mentioned above to access the FileVault tab

2.　　　Click on the lock and enter your administrator password to make changes

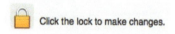

3.　　　Click on the **Turn On FileVault** button and restart your Mac to complete the changes

The only problem with FileVault is that you can't use it to encrypt and send individual files to someone else. Luckily, there is free Mac software you can use to do the job. Let me show you how to encrypt files with AES 256 encryption using an app called Encrypto.

1.　　　Download Encrypto from the Apple App Store and install it

2.　　　Open the app and drag & drop the files you want to encrypt into it. Alternatively, click on the plus sign and add files the way you normally

would

3.　　　Enter a password and a password hint, then click on **Encrypt**

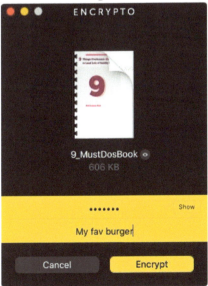

4.   To share the encrypted file, click on the **Share** button and select a sharing method. You can also save the file to your Mac

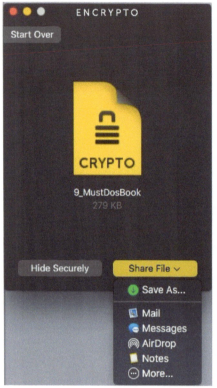

5. To decrypt the file, open it, enter the password you set up for it, then click on Decrypt. The file will be decrypted.

Now you know how to encrypt your files to protect them from prying eyes. This means that we've pretty much covered all you need to know about computer security. There is only one more thing to discuss – security software options for your computer.

Your Weapons Against the Enemy

An Overview of Security Software

Well, now you know a lot about computer security and you should be able to protect yourself from all kinds of online threats. But you will definitely need one thing – security software. Even if you know everything about malware, scams, spam, phishing, identity theft and so on, you will never be 100% safe if you don't use the right software.

There are a lot of security programs that you can use to protect your computer – anti-viruses, anti-malware, anti-spyware, behavioral scanners, personal firewalls and so on. In addition to that, there are various encryption programs that will help you protect your confidential files, file shredders to make sure your deleted files are unrecoverable, and various security add-ons for your browser. Let's have a look at what's available.

Just something I'd like you to know, though. I will not recommend any particular software and say that it's better than the rest for one simple reason – everybody has different needs. So it's unfair to say that one anti-virus is a lot better than the other. Rest assured that I will only list high quality, reputable software that is used and loved by millions of people. So, here goes.

Anti-viruses and Internet security suites for Windows

There are a lot of anti-viruses available for download. Some of them require you to buy a subscription, whereas some of them are free. Generally speaking, the free anti-viruses are just as good as the paid ones. You don't get as many features as with a paid anti-virus, but the existing features work very well. So, here is my list of recommended anti-virus programs:

• **ESET** – ESET is a well-known security software developer. Their anti-virus, NOD32, has been around for years and keeps getting a high rating from independent security experts. In addition to the anti-virus, there is ESET Smart Security (an Internet security suite), ESET Mobile Security for smartphones and ESET Cybersecurity for Mac.

• **BitDefender** – BitDefender is another popular name in the computer security world. This developer offers high-ranking security software with lots of different features. For example, their Total Security suite includes everything you would want from an Internet security program plus a file shredder, encryption, a two-way firewall and even an online backup solution. As for the product range, there is BitDefender Antivirus for both PC and Mac, BitDefender Internet Security, BitDefender Mobile Security for Android, and BitDefender Total Security.

• **Kaspersky** – this security software developer proves that not only viruses originate in Russia. Kaspersky is a respected brand and its security software is used by millions of people and businesses worldwide.

Kaspersky products never fail to perform well in independent tests and are very easy to use. Just like the security software manufacturers mentioned above, Kaspersky offers a wide range of security products for all types of users: Kaspersky PURE Total Security, Kaspersky Internet Security, Kaspersky Anti-Virus for Windows and Mac, and Kaspersky Mobile Security.

• **McAfee** – McAfee is a really big name in the security software industry thanks to its business security solutions and the fact that a lot of laptop manufacturers pre-install the trial version of McAfee antivirus on their laptops. McAfee is a well-respected developer and they offer decent protection. If your laptop came with a trial version of McAfee and you liked it, then there is really no need to look for an alternative anti-virus solution. McAfee's product range includes McAfee All Access (protection for all your devices), McAfee Total Protection, McAfee Internet Security and McAfee AntiVirus Plus. In addition to that, McAfee develops mobile security solutions.

• **Norton** – developed by Symantec, Norton security products are just as well-known as McAfee's. Norton is another popular anti-virus that gets pre-installed by laptop manufacturers. Symantec's security software offers decent protection, but can be heavy on system resources if you have an older and less powerful computer. The most popular Norton products are Norton 360, Norton Internet Security, and Norton AntiVirus.

Free anti-viruses:

I've already mentioned that there are anti-virus programs that are absolutely free for home users. They are often just as good as paid solutions, if not better. So, here are some really good ones for you to try:

• **Windows Defender** – if you are using Windows 8 or Windows 10, then you already have an anti-virus installed on your PC. Back in the days of early versions, most people were disappointed by Microsoft's Windows Defender. But now it's very efficient, so I recommend keeping it enabled. At times it consumes a lot of system resources but that's usually during scans and updates so it doesn't last long. If you're on Windows 7 and earlier, then check out Microsoft Security Essentials. It's only a basic anti-virus program, but it's definitely worth having.

• **Avast! Free Antivirus** – this anti-virus has been an absolute favorite for years. Avast is reliable, its features match the features of many paid anti-viruses, and it's a lot lighter on system resources than, for example, Norton. Avast offers protection against viruses, malware and spyware. The program is free for personal, non-commercial use.

• **Avira AntiVir Free** – Avira is another popular name on the security software market. Their products receive a high rating in independent tests, especially their paid anti-virus. Their free anti-virus product is good too, though. The only annoying thing about it is a pop-up ad that prompts you to upgrade every time the definitions are updated. Otherwise, it's a great free anti-virus.

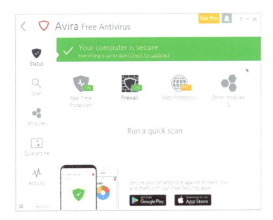

• **AVG AntiVirus Free Edition** – this is the most downloaded free anti-virus program on CNET Download.com. AVG scores really well in independent tests, has features that a lot of free anti-virus programs lack (for example, identity protection), and offers good all-round protection. The only disadvantage of AVG is that it's sometimes heavy on system resources, especially if you have an older computer.

Well, this should do as far as anti-viruses are concerned. Of course there are a lot more programs to choose from, but these are the ones I really like. And now is the time to have a look at Mac solutions.

Anti-viruses and Internet security suites for Mac

As I've already explained, having a Mac doesn't mean you don't need an anti-virus or an Internet security suite that will not only protect your computer, but will also protect your privacy when you are browsing the Web. Here is what's available for Mac OS X for free:

• **Sophos Anti-Virus for Mac Home Edition** - Sophos is a reputable security software developer and their Mac anti-virus is considered to be one of the best. It has a native Mac OS X look and feel, is easy to navigate and, most importantly, does a good job protecting users from all sorts of threats. And best of all, there is a free version.

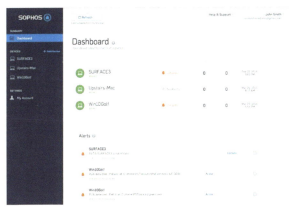

• **Avast! Free Mac Security** - Avast is the developer of one of the most popular free Windows anti-virus programs. Its Mac anti-virus is just as good as the Windows one. It provides comprehensive protection while being fast and unintrusive.

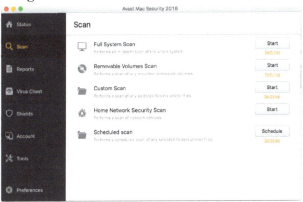

As you can see, there are some really good anti-viruses for Mac that you can use free of charge. Those of you who are still skeptical about using security software on a Mac can stay skeptical. But think of it this way - why not install free security software and have peace of mind rather than not install anything and regret it when malware developers start targeting Mac in earnest.

Third party personal firewalls for Windows

Most Internet Security suites and some anti-viruses have a built-in firewall that will protect your computer from hacker attacks. However, most free anti-viruses do not include a firewall. Of course, you could always use the Windows built-in firewall together with your anti-virus, but if you are looking for something more advanced, here are some personal firewalls for you to consider:

• **ZoneAlarm Free Firewall** – this is an excellent choice for everyone, no matter whether you are a less experienced user or an expert. ZoneAlarm Free Firewall is an inbound/outbound operating system firewall solution that does a great job protecting your system from intruders. ZoneAlarm is also very easy to configure and use.

• **Comodo Firewall** – this is another great choice for those wanting to protect their computer from intruders. Comodo Firewall has all the features that are normally present in paid solutions, provides proactive protection, and offers flexible customization options.

• **Private Firewall** – another freebie offering multilayer intrusion protection. This software combines a personal firewall with protection against viruses, malware and spyware. It also offers registry protection, IP filtering, system anomaly detection and more. All for free.

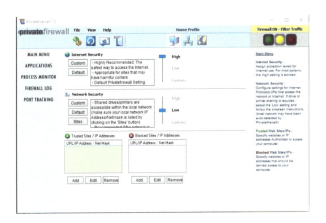

Now that you have a firewall, let's look at anti-malware and anti-spyware programs. Also let's have a good look at free zero-day threat protection programs.

Anti-malware, anti-spyware and zero-day threat protection for Windows

Most anti-viruses offer protection against all kinds of malware and against spyware. However, it's always best to use specifically developed software to remove malware, as anti-viruses often miss infections like Trojans, worms and spyware programs.

On top of that, anti-viruses are not great when it comes to protection against zero-day threats. Luckily, there are several free anti-malware programs you can use:

• **Malwarebytes Anti-Malware** – this is by far the best anti-malware program available today. If your anti-virus misses an infection, Malwarebytes will find it. It's a really powerful tool that can find and remove just about any piece of malware. Malwarebytes doesn't offer live protection, so you shouldn't use it instead of a real-time anti-virus scanner. But it's a great addition to your arsenal of security software. A real must-have.

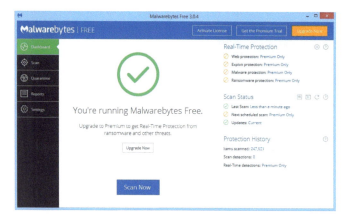

• **Hitman Pro Alert** – this is another good tool for monitoring your PC against threats. It's an ideal program for nipping infections in the bud.

Browser security add-ons

It's not a secret that infections come from the Internet and that your browsers are among the most vulnerable pieces of software on your computer. Even Mac's Safari is considered hugely unsafe and was the cause of the most recent attacks on Mac computers. This means that you should give your browsers some extra attention and make sure they are well protected.

Your security software should patch up quite a few browser vulnerabilities. But you would be better off getting programs that specialize in browser security. I'm talking about different security and privacy add-ons and extensions. There are lots of them available for download in Chrome Store, through Mozilla and there are security add-ons for Internet Explorer too.

Here is a short list of add-ons that will help you stay safe:

• **Redirect Remover** – an exceptionally useful add-on that prevents browser hijackers from redirecting you to malicious websites.

• **Web of Trust (WOT)** – this add-on is compatible with Internet Explorer, Firefox and Chrome. Basically, it's a community-powered tool that shows you the rating for websites in Google search and when you visit them. If a website is known to contain malicious script, WOT will notify you and thus help you stay away from malware.

• **Adblock Plus** – this add-on is available for Internet Explorer, Firefox and Chrome. What it does is block ads based on predefined patterns. Not only does it make browsing more pleasant, but it also protects you from ads that lead to malicious websites.

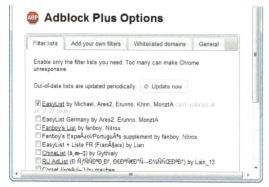

• **NoScript** – this is a very useful add-on for Firefox that blocks malicious script and only allows Java and JavaScript content from trusted websites. Chrome users should consider installing NoScript.

• **LastPass** – a browser add-on that acts as a password manager. This add-on is compatible with Internet Explorer, Firefox and Chrome. It also supports mobile operating systems, such as iOS, Android, Symbian and BlackBerry. This add-on stores your passwords in encrypted form, thus allowing you to use strong passwords without the risk of forgetting or losing them.

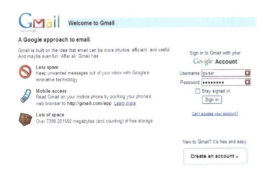

• **Better Privacy** – this Firefox add-on does a great job protecting you from tracking cookies. It manages to block tracking cookies that can't be blocked or deleted by any other means.

• **SaferChrome** - this is a really useful add-on that detects if a website transmits your private information, such as passwords and credit card numbers, as plain text (no website should ever do this). Websites should encrypt the information you enter to protect you and not practically broadcast it. If you are browsing a website and SaferChrome tells you that it doesn't encrypt your details, you should think twice about using the website in the future.

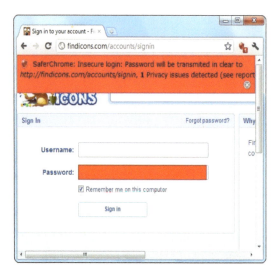

Now your computer should be protected from all sorts of threats. You should have all the software to keep your PC or Mac safe. But I'd like to remind you one more time that nothing can protect you from viruses, malware and spyware better than your common sense. Remember that when it comes to computer security, it's good to be suspicious.

Conclusion

As you can see, it's not all that hard to maintain computer security and keep your private data safe from prying eyes. At least if you are a home user (businesses have a lot more to worry about). Fundamentally, all you need to do is follow some basic security rules, install good anti-virus and anti-malware software, and use your common sense. The most important thing is that now you know your enemy and have the knowledge that will help you fight and avoid online and offline threats.

Now you know what kind of threats are out there and you know how to counter them. You've learned how to ensure secure access to your system and protect your wireless network from unauthorized access. We've also covered viruses, malware, Trojans, worms, keyloggers, rootkits, spyware and other infections that lurk around. You've also learned which security software to install, so that your computer stays infection-free.

In addition to everything mentioned above, you now know how to behave online, what not to do and what sort of information you should never share. Moreover, you know how to identify scams and fraud, and how to protect your online accounts. Basically, you know everything a home user should know to keep safe online. Trust me, this knowledge is more important and more valuable than dozens of anti-virus programs because safe browsing habits are a 98% guarantee that you will never-ever get infected.

And now my last bit of advice. Remember that malware and scams keep evolving every minute. Never lose your vigilance and remember that being suspicious when it comes to things happening online is always a good thing. Keep your shields up and enjoy a virus-free, secure computer!

About the author

Liz Cornwell has written several non-fiction books on a variety of subjects. She is a well-known computer optimization expert and has established a reputation for understanding the needs of her readers, providing easy-to-follow advice and technical accuracy.

Coming from a non-technical background, Liz Cornwell knows how frustrating computers can be. She's also aware of the fact that reading about computers and using them is not the same thing. That's why Liz writes her books in a plain, non-technical language that makes complicated things easy to understand. The goal of her books is to get people started and help them get the most out of their PCs.

www.ingramcontent.com/pod-product-compliance
Lightning Source LLC
Chambersburg PA
CBHW041141050326
40689CB00001B/439